A Slow Walk in a House Divided

A Slow Walk in a House Divided

70 Devotional Meditations on 1 Kings and 2 Kings

Edward B. Allen

Melbourne

A Slow Walk in a House Divided:
70 Devotional Meditations on 1 Kings and 2 Kings
by Edward B. Allen
Copyright © 2023 by Edward B. Allen
All rights reserved worldwide.

Published by Edward B. Allen
Melbourne, Florida
Email: edward.allen1949@gmail.com

ISBN: 979-8-9875875-0-8 (paperback)
979-8-9875875-1-5 (ebook *.epub)
979-8-9875875-2-2 (Kindle ebook)

Cover design by Raney Day Creative, LLC.

To Angie

Contents

Contents

Preface

What does Bible history have to do with a Christan's spiritual walk today? The books of First Kings and Second Kings[1] in the Bible describe people and events from an ancient culture which was very different from our world today. Ancient Israel and Judah were also spiritually different from the church today. I know how to apply personal poetry like Psalms to my life, but history?

However, the God of King David is the same today as back then. The books of 1 Kings and 2 Kings are part of the Word of God. They are in the Bible for us. This book's purpose is to find spiritual applications of the stories in 1 Kings and 2 Kings for today's Christian.

When applying the lessons of 1 Kings and 2 Kings, I look for warnings for churches and individuals today. If something was sin in ancient Israel and Judah, then similar things are sin today. If someone was a bad example, then I know what to avoid in my life. If someone was a good example, then I can imitate them.

Some commentaries on 1 Kings and 2 Kings analyze the history of Israel and Judah in the context of Middle East history. Others emphasize the main theological message of the books. Instead of analyzing history or theology, this book consists of devotional meditations. The modern illustrations are based on the recollections of actual people and events by friends, family, or myself unless otherwise indicated.

Even though this is not an academic book, I have benefited greatly from Christian scholars. Some historical and cultural information is from a commentary by Richard D. Patterson and

---

[1]First Kings is referenced by 1 Kings, and Second Kings is referenced by 2 Kings.

Hermann J. Austel.[2] Unfortunately, it is not practical to cite all the pastors and books from whom I have gleaned over the years.

The Christian Standard Bible (CSB) is quoted as the primary translation. It is a modern translation based on the latest evangelical Bible scholarship. Clarifications of quotations are in [brackets]. Scripture references consist of book, chapter, verses, and version (if relevant), for example, "John 3:16 (CSB)."

A word or phrase referred to as a word is in *italics*. Male pronouns are sometimes used to indicate a person of either gender. All Scripture references and section titles are indexed.

I am thankful for the helpful comments by Ron Chambers, Pam King, Fred Monett and Angie Allen. I am also thankful for the steadfast support of my wife Angie.

E.B.A.

[2]Richard D. Patterson and Hermann J. Austel, "1, 2 Kings," *The Expositor's Bible Commentary: 1 Kings–Job*, Volume 4 (Grand Rapids, Michigan: Zondervan, 1988).

1

A house divided

The bumper sticker on the car ahead of me said "A House Divided." When I got closer, I realized that the husband and wife were loyal to rival college football teams. Somehow they got married anyway. When it came to football, their family was a "house divided."

The twelve tribes of Israel were a united kingdom under Saul, David, and Solomon. After Solomon's death, the kingdom split in two—a house divided. Ten tribes to the north formed the kingdom of Israel, and the tribes of Judah and Benjamin formed the kingdom of Judah.[1] Chapter 12 of 1 Kings through the end of 2 Kings traces the history of these two kingdoms up to when they were conquered and the people were deported. Israel was deported by Assyria and Judah was deported by Babylon.

Rather than focus on the details of their history, this book presents devotional meditations from the era of the house divided. When I read the Bible, even the history books, I want to apply God's truths to my life. The books of 1 Kings and 2 Kings

---

[1] Jacob had twelve sons who were ancestors to the tribes of Israelites. When Joshua allocated the land of Canaan to the Israelites, the tribe of Levi was supposed to live among the other tribes and were not allocated an area. Joseph's descendants had become two tribes, Ephraim and Manasseh, who were each allocated land, for a total of twelve tribes allocated land. Even though Simeon's allocation of land was in southern Canaan, the tribe of Simeon apparently lived among the northern tribes by the time of the kings. J. Barton Payne, "1, 2 Chronicles," *The Expositor's Bible Commentary: 1 Kings–Job*, Volume 4 (Grand Rapids, Michigan: Zondervan, 1988), p. 343.

provide examples of good and evil people and God's assessment of their actions. Wherever my life is similar to an example or the opposite, I can apply the message.

Solomon's legacy

A *legacy* is something handed down from one's ancestors. When my father died, I remembered the life lessons he had taught me. Those lessons were much more valuable than the possessions I inherited. When Solomon died, the condition of his kingdom was the legacy he passed to his son.

> When Solomon was old, his wives turned his heart away to follow other gods. He was not wholeheartedly devoted to the Lord his God, as his father David had been.
>
> 1 Kings 11:4 (CSB)

Solomon married hundreds of foreign women for his harem.[2] In his later years, to please them, he built places for worship of their foreign gods, and he worshiped the idols with his wives. Marrying foreign wives was forbidden by the law of Moses precisely because it would lead to worship like the pagan nations. The people followed Solomon's example. Consequently, the Lord allowed military opponents to attack Solomon's kingdom. Worshiping idols was so offensive to the Lord that he also told Solomon the kingdom would be divided during his son's reign.

If a believer is not careful, those he loves can influence him so his love for the Lord grows cold. Solomon loved his wives, but they led him astray. Jesus reproved the church in Ephesus for abandoning their love for him.[3]

> But I have this against you: You have abandoned the love you had at first. Remember then how far you have fallen; repent, and do the works you did at first.

---

[2]1 Kings 11:1–25.
[3]Revelation 2:1–7.

Otherwise, I will come to you and remove your lamp-stand from its place, unless you repent.

Revelation 2:4–5 (CSB)

Even though the church in Ephesus had many good qualities, Jesus called for them to repent and turn back to him. I must keep my love for the Lord fresh, no matter what my loved ones think, so I don't end up like Solomon. Solomon left a legacy of idol worship in the land. I want to leave a legacy of devotion to the Lord.

PRAYER: Lord, help me keep my love for you fresh. Amen.

Ahijah, prophet from Shiloh

Jeroboam, son of Nebat, was a young manager for Solomon who was in charge of laborers from Ephraim and Manasseh. They worked on a big government project in Jerusalem.

During that time, the prophet Ahijah the Shilonite met Jeroboam on the road as Jeroboam came out of Jerusalem. Now Ahijah had wrapped himself with a new cloak, and the two of them were alone in the open field. Then Ahijah took hold of the new cloak he had on, [and] tore it into twelve pieces.

1 Kings 11:29–30 (CSB)

The Lord gave a message to the prophet Ahijah from Shiloh for Jeroboam.[4] Ahijah met Jeroboam on the road in private and delivered his message in dramatic fashion, tearing his cloak into pieces representing the twelve tribes of Israel. The Lord promised Jeroboam a kingdom consisting of ten tribes. The Lord also promised Jeroboam a lasting dynasty if he would remain loyal to the Lord. When Solomon found out about the prophecy, Jeroboam fled to Egypt until Solomon's death.

---

[4]1 Kings 11:26–40.

I wonder what Ahijah thought about the prophecy he was supposed to give Jeroboam. He was probably grieved to see Solomon's legacy of idol worship. Dividing the kingdom didn't seem like a good thing either. Ahijah knew his job was just to obey the Lord and deliver the message to Jeroboam.

When the Holy Spirit nudges me to say or do something, I just have to do it, like Ahijah did.

> If anyone speaks, let it be as one who speaks God's words; if anyone serves, let it be from the strength God provides, so that God may be glorified through Jesus Christ in everything. To him be the glory and the power forever and ever. Amen.
>
> 1 Peter 4:11 (CSB)

I don't try to act like an Old Testament prophet proclaiming, "Thus says the Lord!" I just speak normally. It is foolish to try to figure out what the Lord wants to accomplish or how he will do it. Sometimes the message is intended for someone who overhears the conversation, rather than the person I'm talking to. Sometimes a simple act of service speaks louder than words. The Lord takes simple conversations and produces amazing results.

> PRAYER: Lord, I want to do whatever you tell me to do or say. Thank you for producing spiritual results. Amen.

Rebellious Israelites

In AD 1776, thirteen colonies declared their independence from a foolish and stubborn king who was thirty-eight years old. In 931 BC, ten tribes declared their independence from a foolish and stubborn king who was forty-one years old.

> Then the king [Rehoboam] answered the people harshly. He rejected the advice the elders had given him and spoke to them according to the young men's advice: "My father made your yoke heavy, but I will

4

add to your yoke; my father disciplined you with whips, but I will discipline you with [scorpions]." ...

When all Israel saw that the king had not listened to them, the people answered him:
What portion do we have in David?
We have no inheritance in the son of Jesse.
Israel, return to your tents;
David, now look after your own house!
So Israel went to their tents.

1 Kings 12:13–16 (CSB)

Solomon's son Rehoboam went to Shechem to be crowned king over a united Israel.[5] Because Solomon had conscripted laborers for government projects, the people asked Rehoboam for a lighter workload. He rejected the advice of his father's officials and adopted the advice of his childhood friends. He promised harsher treatment than his father had imposed. The ten northern tribes rejected Rehoboam as king.

Judah remained loyal to David's dynasty, because David was from Judah. Benjamin was allied with Judah also.

Rehoboam's reply to the people was arrogant and foolish. He thought he could bully them into submission.

Jesus was different. Even though he is the Son of God, he was humble and gentle. As his disciple, I must imitate my master, learning to be humble in all my relationships.

When a leader is arrogant and foolish, it is natural to protest and complain. The people of Israel were rebellious. When I'm faced with poor leadership, I can't rebel. I must pray.

First of all, then, I urge that petitions, prayers, intercessions, and thanksgivings be made for everyone, for kings and all those who are in authority, so that we may lead a tranquil and quiet life in all godliness and dignity.

1 Timothy 2:1–2 (CSB)

---

[5] 1 Kings 12:1–17.

The New Testament teaches us to pray for those in authority.[6] In the First Century, praying for those in authority even included the pagan Roman emperors.

> PRAYER: Lord, I will pray for the President and other officials, my boss at work, and my pastor. Amen.

When did the kings reign?

The house divided began when Israel rejected Rehoboam, Solomon's son, as king, in about 931 BC and continued for almost 350 years. The northern kingdom of Israel ended in 722 BC, and the southern kingdom of Judah ended in 586 BC.

Precise dating of the reigns of the kings of Israel and Judah is controversial among Bible scholars. They analyze a variety of biblical and historical data. The dates provided by Patterson and Austel[7] are sufficient for our purposes. Overlapping reigns occur when a father and son ruled together in coregency. Reigns may begin or end in a partial year. Some Bible passages use an alternative name for a king. A few kings had the same name as another king; they are distinguished by their fathers' names.

The following lists kings in chronological order of when they began to reign, noting which kingdom and the years of their reigns.

Kings of Israel and Judah

King of Israel	Reign (years BC)	King of Judah	Reign (years BC)
Jeroboam	931–910	Rehoboam	931–914
		Abijam	913–910
Nadab	910–909		
Baasha	909–886	Asa	909–868
Elah	886–885		
Zimri	885 (7 days)		
Omri	885–874		

---

[6]See also 1 Peter 2:13–17.
[7]Patterson and Austel, p. 13.

Kings of Israel and Judah (continued)

King of Israel	Reign (years BC)	King of Judah	Reign (years BC)
Ahab	874–853		
		Jehoshaphat	872–847
Ahaziah	853–852		
Joram (also called Jehoram)	852–841	Jehoram	852–841
		Ahaziah	841 (one year)
Jehu	841–814	Athaliah (mother of Ahaziah)	841–835
		Joash	835–796
Jehoahaz	814–798		
Jehoash	798–782		
		Amaziah	796–767
Jeroboam	793–753		
		Azariah (also called Uzziah)	791–739
Zechariah	753 (6 months)		
Shallum	752 (one month)	Jotham	752–736
Menahem	751–742		
Pekahiah	741–740		
Pekah	740–732		
		Ahaz	736–720
Hoshea	732–722		
		Hezekiah	729–699
		Manasseh	698–643
		Amon	642–640
		Josiah	640–609
		Jehoahaz	609 (3 months)
		Jehoiakim	609–598
		Jehoiachin	598 (3 months)
		Zedekiah	597–586

7

2

The era of Jeroboam's dynasty (931–909 BC)

Most rulers want a dynasty. They want their children, grand-children, and descendants to have the same power they have wielded. They want their family to be famous in history.

Modern political dynasties are unusual. Perhaps the Bush family is the most prominent recent example. Prescott Sheldon Bush (1895–1972) served as a U.S. Senator. His son, George Herbert Walker Bush (1924–2018) was elected President of the United States in 1988. His son, George Walker Bush (born 1946), was elected President in 2000. His younger brother, J.E.B. Bush (born 1953), served as governor of Florida and unsuccessfully ran for President in 2016. People wondered if voters would continue the dynasty. His son, George Prescott Bush (born 1976), was elected commissioner of the Texas General Land Office. Again, people wondered if voters would continue the dynasty in higher office.

This chapter includes devotional meditations on the following: Jeroboam and his son, kings of Israel; kings of Judah who began their reigns during this time; and a couple of others. This era ended when Jeroboam's son Nadab was assassinated.

Rehoboam, son of Solomon, King of Judah

The company where I worked had an organization chart showing who was the supervisor of each unit in the company. Whenever a new top manager was hired, the company was completely re-organized and a new organization chart was distributed. I had a hard time keeping up with all the organization charts.

Rehoboam reigned in Judah from about 931 to 914 BC. When Israel rebelled, he had to reorganize his kingdom. Some of his building projects had to be canceled. However, the religious organization chart from his father's reign was not affected.

> Judah [during the reign of Rehoboam] did what was evil in the Lord's sight. They provoked him to jealous anger more than all that their ancestors had done with the sins they committed. They also built for themselves high places, sacred pillars, and Asherah poles on every high hill and under every green tree; there were even male cult prostitutes in the land. They imitated all the detestable practices of the nations the Lord had dispossessed before the Israelites.
>
> 1 Kings 14:22–24 (CSB)

Rehoboam continued Solomon's idolatry, adding to the shrines in high places which had sacred stone idols and poles dedicated to the fertility goddess Asherah. The people worshiped the Lord in Jerusalem and worshiped like ancient Canaanites on hilltops.

Secular society today tempts with many things that are like ancient idols, such as money, career, sports, hobbies, fame, sexuality, drugs, influence, and political power. For example, Paul told the Ephesians that greed for money is idolatry and sexual immorality is just as bad.

> For know and recognize this: Every sexually immoral or impure or greedy person, who is an idolater, does not have an inheritance in the kingdom of Christ and of God.
>
> Ephesians 5:5 (CSB)

10

It is easy to worship the Lord on Sunday and be loyal to other things during the week. Loyalty to anything ahead of the Lord God is evil. Temptations of society are all around me. I must cling to the Lord above all else.

> PRAYER: Lord, help me to recognize the temptations around me and to reject them. Amen.

Jeroboam, son of Nebat, King of Israel

I worked with some engineers who wanted to be managers. They started wearing suits to work every day like managers did. They worked hard to bring in big contracts and eventually formed their own company. They were ambitious like Jeroboam.

The northern ten tribes chose Jeroboam to be their king. This fulfilled the prophecy by Ahijah, the prophet from Shiloh. Jeroboam reigned in Israel from about 931 to 910 BC.

> [King Jeroboam] made two golden calves, and he said to the people, "Going to Jerusalem is too difficult for you. Israel, here are your gods who brought you up from the land of Egypt." He set up one in Bethel, and put the other in Dan. This led to sin; the people walked in procession before one of the calves all the way to Dan.
>
> 1 Kings 12:28–30 (CSB)

To prevent his people from worshiping the Lord in Jerusalem in the southern kingdom, Jeroboam set up golden calf idols in Bethel and Dan for the people to worship. He also built shrines, chose priests, and established a festival, all contrary to the law of Moses.

Ambitious leaders sometimes try to boost their influence by giving people a religion that they invented.

> There were indeed false prophets among the [Israelite] people, just as there will be false teachers among you. They will bring in destructive heresies, even denying

the Master who bought them, and will bring swift destruction on themselves. Many will follow their depraved ways, and the way of truth will be maligned because of them. They will exploit you in their greed with made-up stories. Their condemnation, pronounced long ago, is not idle, and their destruction does not sleep.

2 Peter 2:1–3 (CSB)

False teaching may be bright and shiny. It may sound smooth. It may be convenient. But idols are not God. Being popular does not make a false teaching true. False teaching is often motivated by greed, another idol. I must always evaluate whether religious leaders are teaching the truth or stories they made up.

PRAYER: Lord, I know faith is the only way to have a relationship with you. Amen.

Jeroboam rebuked

Jeroboam's golden calf idols in Bethel and Dan outraged the Lord, so he sent a prophet from Judah to Bethel.

A man of God came, however, from Judah to Bethel by the word of the Lord while Jeroboam was standing beside the altar to burn incense. The man of God cried out against the altar by the word of the Lord: "Altar, altar, this is what the Lord says, 'A son will be born to the house of David, named Josiah, and he will sacrifice on you the priests of the high places who are burning incense on you. Human bones will be burned on you.' "

1 Kings 13:1–2 (CSB)

The prophet cursed the altar Jeroboam had set up and predicted who would desecrate it, namely King Josiah of Judah. This prophecy was fulfilled over three hundred years later.[1]

---

[1]The Scriptures do not give precise dates for these events.

When Jeroboam heard this rebuke, he pointed at the prophet to arrest him, but his hand was paralyzed (withered) and the altar was ripped apart. He asked the prophet to pray to the Lord to heal his hand, and the Lord did so. Jeroboam may have repented from arresting the prophet, but in spite of the miraculous signs, he did not turn from his idolatry.

When I fall into sin, the Lord's love reaches out to me like he did to Jeroboam. He corrects me with word and circumstances. Sometimes I'm stubborn and half hearted like Jeroboam. God has a solution to my sin.

> If we confess our sins, [God] is faithful and righteous to forgive us our sins and to cleanse us from all unrighteousness.
>
> 1 John 1:9 (CSB)

He has promised to forgive my sin if I will just repent. He will cleanse me of all my unrighteousness. Then I am prepared to do what he says.

> PRAYER: Lord, thank you for forgiving all of my sins. Amen.

Man of God from Judah

When my wife and I were about to move out of state, we sold our house before I could leave my job. A couple in our church, invited us into their home for the ten days we were homeless. We appreciated their hospitality and fellowship. The man of God from Judah was offered hospitality too.

The prophet who had cursed the altar in Bethel promptly left town to return home. When an old prophet in Bethel heard about what had happened, he got on his donkey to catch up with the prophet from Judah.

> Then [the old prophet from Bethel] said to [the man of God from Judah], "Come home with me and eat some food."

But he answered, "I cannot go back with you or accompany you; I will not eat food or drink water with
you in this place. For a message came to me by the
word of the Lord: 'You must not eat food or drink water there or go back by the way you came.' "

He said to him, "I am also a prophet like you. An
angel spoke to me by the word of the Lord: 'Bring him
back with you to your house so that he may eat food
and drink water.' " The old prophet deceived him,
and the man of God went back with him, ate food in
his house, and drank water.

1 Kings 13:15–19 (CSB)

When the old prophet found the prophet from Judah on the
road, he invited him to dinner. When the prophet from Judah
declined, the old prophet deceived him, claiming to have a more
recent word from the Lord. So they had dinner together.

During dinner the Lord gave a genuine word to the old prophet, reproving the prophet from Judah for disobedience. He
said, "Your corpse will never reach the grave of your ancestors."
After dinner, the prophet from Judah started home. On the way,
he was killed by a lion. The old prophet buried him in his personal grave in Bethel.

Like the old prophet from Bethel, sometimes other people
think they know what God wants me to do. They have good
intentions. For example, a grandmother at church said to me,
"You should marry my granddaughter." I listened politely, but
I never met her granddaughter. I must obey the leading of the
Holy Spirit.

For all those led by God's Spirit are God's sons.

Romans 8:14 (CSB)

If advice is from the Lord, the Holy Spirit will confirm it in
my heart. Like the prophet from Judah, I must hear from God for
myself.

PRAYER: Lord, I am always listening for your direction. Amen.

Jeroboam's wife

Every mother worries about the health of her children. When a child dies, the grief can be overwhelming and lasts a lifetime.

One of Jeroboam's sons was sick, so he sent the boy's mother to the prophet Ahijah to find out whether he would get well. Naturally, she was concerned for her son.

> [Jeroboam's wife] went to Shiloh and arrived at Ahijah's house. Ahijah could not see; he was blind due to his age. But the Lord had said to Ahijah, "Jeroboam's wife is coming soon to ask you about her son, for he is sick. You are to say such and such to her. When she arrives, she will be disguised."
>
> When Ahijah heard the sound of her feet entering the door, he said, "Come in, wife of Jeroboam! Why are you disguised? I have bad news for you..."
>
> Then Jeroboam's wife got up and left and went to Tirzah. As she was crossing the threshold of the house, the boy died. He was buried, and all Israel mourned for him, according to the word of the Lord he had spoken through his servant the prophet Ahijah.
>
> 1 Kings 14:4–18 (CSB)

When she arrived, Ahijah immediately prophesied against Jeroboam's dynasty, because of the idolatry he had introduced to Israel. He predicted every male would be killed. He also predicted that the boy would die as soon as his mother returned home. The boy's death was a sign that the rest of Ahijah's prophecy was true.

I wonder what Jeroboam's wife thought about as she returned home. She was probably grieved by the news her son would die. She may have thought about all the idols people were worshiping throughout Israel. When her husband needed answers, he sent her to a prophet of the Lord, not an idol's prophet.

Whenever I need answers, I won't rely on my friends' opinions. I can't rely on popular social media. Secular advice is based on human wisdom and is often based on modern "idols."

> Now if any of you lacks wisdom, he should ask God—
> who gives to all generously and ungrudgingly—and
> it will be given to him. But let him ask in faith with-
> out doubting. For the doubter is like the surging sea,
> driven and tossed by the wind.
>
> James 1:5–6 (CSB)

For example, I eagerly started a project on my own. Then suddenly I realized I needed God's wisdom. I repented for rushing
ahead. I paused, prayed, and waited for a word from the Holy
Spirit.

When I need answers, I will go to the Lord in prayer for godly
wisdom. The Lord is generous. He promises to give wisdom to
those who ask him for it. I am confident he will answer. I just
need to be alert for his voice.

A wise pastor once said, "Prepare with pre-prayer."

> PRAYER: Lord, please give me your wisdom for every
> task in daily life. Amen.

Abijam, son of Rehoboam, King of Judah

When one does genealogy research, one often finds stories of both
good and not-so-good people among one's ancestors. I have ancestors who were pastors, farmers, engineers, and soldiers. Abijam[2] had King David, Israel's best king, as an ancestor.

Abijam became king when Rehoboam, his father, died. Abijam reigned in Judah from about 913 to 910 BC.

> [King Abijam] walked in all the sins his father before
> him had committed, and he was not wholeheartedly
> devoted to the Lord his God as his ancestor David had
> been.
>
> 1 Kings 15:3 (CSB)

---

[2]Abijam is also called Abijah in 2 Chronicles.

Abijam supported the same Canaanite idolatry as his father Rehoboam. Abijam could have imitated his great grandfather, King David, but instead, he followed the example of his father. It was easy. The people of Judah were already worshiping like Canaanites.

Paul advised those in Philippi to put into practice what they learned from him, their spiritual father.

> Do what you have learned and received and heard from me, and seen in me, and the God of peace will be with you.
>
> Philippians 4:9 (CSB)

When I was about six years, old my father was offended by something at church and never went to church for the rest of his life. My parents never explained what happened. If he had complained about it, I could have inherited his offense. However, I inherited a love for church people from my mother. As I remember my heritage from my parents and grandparents, I will follow the good examples rather than the bad.

> PRAYER: Lord, thank you for the good spiritual heritage from my ancestors. Amen.

Nadab, son of Jeroboam, King of Israel

When a grown child inherits the family business, the first priority is just to keep it going. Immediately making radical changes is usually not advisable. The kingdom was Nadab's family business, and he had to keep it going.

Nadab became king when Jeroboam, his father, died. Nadab reigned in Israel for less than two years from about 910 to 909 BC. He was assassinated.

> [King Nadab] did what was evil in the Lord's sight and walked in the ways of his father and the sin he had caused Israel to commit.
>
> 1 Kings 15:26 (CSB)

Nadab had barely begun to reign in Israel when he was assassinated. During his short reign, he continued worship of the gold calves at Bethel and Dan.

A grown child like Nadab often continues patterns learned from his parents, especially if he inherits the family business. His ambition will be to imitate the success of his father.

> Do nothing out of selfish ambition or conceit, but in humility consider others as more important than yourselves.
>
> Philippians 2:3 (CSB)

As a teenager, my father and I raced a small sailboat. It was a lot of fun. I wanted to race sailboats for the rest of my life, but then I realized that most sailing races are held on Sundays. That would prevent me from worshiping with other Christians. I have had to give up ambitions that distracted me from the Lord, even those I learned from my parents.

PRAYER: Lord, help me recognize my selfish ambitions, so I can give them up. Amen.

3

The era of Baasha's dynasty (909–885 BC)

In American politics, the transition from one major party to the other one may not be violent, but it is not peaceful. Emotions run hot. In ancient times, the transition from one dynasty to another was usually violent. For example, Julius Caesar overthrew the Roman Senate in a civil war. "Crossing the Rubicon" river was his declaration of war. Baasha's dynasty replaced Jeroboam's.

This chapter includes devotional meditations on the following: Baasha and his son Elah, kings of Israel; Zimri, who assassinated Elah; Asa who reigned in Judah throughout this time; and the prophet Jehu. This era ended when Zimri committed suicide.

Baasha, son of Ahijah, King of Israel

On November 22, 1963, John F. Kennedy, President of the United States, was assassinated. His Vice-President, Lyndon B. Johnson became president. Those who heard the news that day were shocked. Kennedy's assassin was himself assassinated a short while later. Baasha was an assassin.

Baasha[1] reigned in Israel from about 909 to 886 BC.

---

[1]Baasha was not the son of Ahijah, the prophet from Shiloh.

Baasha son of Ahijah of the house of Issachar con-
spired against Nadab, and Baasha struck him down
at Gibbethon of the Philistines while Nadab and all
Israel were besieging Gibbethon. In the third year of
Judah's King Asa, Baasha killed Nadab and reigned in
his place.

1 Kings 15:27–28 (CSB)

Baasha killed King Nadab while the king was with the army
besieging a Philistine town. He must have had co-conspirators
in the army. Then he seized the throne. Baasha was the first to
assassinate a king in Israel or Judah.

Office politics today can have conspiracies like Baasha's. Even
though the boss may not be murdered, people often plot and
scheme to replace him. Ambition and greed lead to hatred.
Church politics can be just as bad.

Everyone who hates his brother or sister is a murderer,
and you know that no murderer has eternal life resid-
ing in him.

1 John 3:15 (CSB)

Hatred is morally equivalent to murder. Hating the boss at
the office is like Baasha assassinating the king. I am determined
to not let hatred gain a foothold in my life.

PRAYER: Lord, help me keep a good attitude when I
encounter an oppressive boss. Amen.

Jehu, son of Hanani, prophet of the Lord

Sometimes the boss at work will tell me to give a message to
someone else in the office. He is the boss, so I deliver the message, "The boss said such and such."

Jehu, the prophet, delivered a message from the Lord to King
Baasha. He predicted Baasha's dynasty would be completely destroyed just like Baasha had destroyed the dynasty of Jeroboam.

Now the word of the Lord came to Jehu son of Hanani against Baasha: "Because I raised you up from the dust and made you ruler over my people Israel, but you have walked in the ways of Jeroboam and have caused my people Israel to sin, angering me with their sins, take note: I will eradicate Baasha and his house, and I will make your house like the house of Jeroboam son of Nebat:
Anyone who belongs to Baasha and dies in the city, the dogs will eat,
and anyone who is his and dies in the field, the birds will eat."

1 Kings 16:1–4 (CSB)

Jehu had an unpleasant and dangerous task. He had to tell the king that all his descendants will be killed. Jehu didn't know how the king would react, but he was obedient. Apparently, he did not suffer any repercussions.

It's always awkward to give someone bad news. In awkward situations, I pray for the spiritual strength to do the right thing.

May our Lord Jesus Christ himself and God our Father, who has loved us and given us eternal encouragement and good hope by grace, encourage your hearts and strengthen you in every good work and word.

2 Thessalonians 2:16–17 (CSB)

I never had to reprimand a king like Jehu did, but one time I had to tell my department head I would not falsify my time card. He wanted me to charge a contract for proposal work (overhead) I was doing. I wondered what his reaction would be. Knowing the Lord is a source of courage for difficult situations. I have to remind myself that the Lord's grace will be there in the aftermath.

PRAYER: Lord, thank you for courage and grace in difficult situations. Amen.

21

Asa, son of Abijam, King of Judah

King David was considered an ideal king, because his heart was dedicated to the Lord. He was not perfect, but when he sinned, he repented. Many of the Psalms testify to us what was in his heart. Asa was like David.

When Abijam died, his son Asa became king. Asa reigned in Judah from about 909 to 868 BC.[2]

> Asa did what was right in the Lord's sight, as his ancestor David had done. He banished the male cult prostitutes from the land and removed all of the idols that his ancestors had made. He also removed his grandmother Maacah from being queen mother because she had made an obscene image of Asherah. Asa chopped down her obscene image and burned it in the Kidron Valley. The high places were not taken away, but Asa was wholeheartedly devoted to the Lord his entire life.
>
> 1 Kings 15:11–14 (CSB)

Rather than continue the pagan practices of his father and grandfather, Asa was like his great great grandfather, King David. He removed from Judah the cult prostitutes and idols his grandfather and father had set up. He even deposed his grandmother from the important office of queen mother and removed her idol of Asherah, the fertility goddess. Even though the shrines on hilltops were allowed to remain, he was commended for his dedication to the Lord.

Sometimes I have had to give up attitudes I may have inherited from my ancestors, like the idols Asa got rid of.

> Be careful that no one takes you captive through philosophy and empty deceit based on human tradition, based on the elements of the world, rather than Christ.
>
> Colossians 2:8 (CSB)

---

[2]Dating kings precisely is difficult and controversial.

While having dinner with my grandmother in the 1960s, I realized she was prejudiced against poor people. It was a common attitude in that era. I had to examine my own heart. Did I feel the same way? I had to turn away from worldly traditions.

> PRAYER: Lord, help me reject worldly traditions, even those my family clings to. Amen.

Elah, son of Baasha, King of Israel

Political leaders must always be alert for conspiracies by ambitious challengers. Modern conspiracies try to influence public opinion through TV and social media on the Internet. In ancient times, a conspiracy could be deadly. Elah was the victim of a conspiracy.

When Baasha died, his son Elah became king. Elah reigned less than two years in Israel from about 886 to 885 BC. He was assassinated.

> [King Elah's] servant Zimri, commander of half his chariots, conspired against him while Elah was in Tirzah getting drunk in the house of Arza, who was in charge of the household at Tirzah. In the twenty-seventh year of Judah's King Asa, Zimri went in and struck Elah down, killing him. Then Zimri became king in his place.
>
> 1 Kings 16:9–10 (CSB)

A high ranking soldier betrayed Elah and ended the dynasty of his father Baasha. Elah was more interested in a party than in protecting his kingdom.

Modern society offers entertainment wherever you turn. Some kinds of entertainment lead to drunkenness, like Elah's party. Some soak up hours and hours.

> Pay careful attention, then, to how you walk—not as unwise people but as wise—making the most of the time, because the days are evil. So don't be foolish,

but understand what the Lord's will is. And don't get drunk with wine, which leads to reckless living, but be filled by the Spirit.

Ephesians 5:15–18 (CSB)

It takes discernment from the Holy Spirit to find the right balance between innocent entertainment and the rest of life. I am always looking for God's tasks for me. They are more important than my entertainment.

PRAYER: Lord, give me discernment regarding your tasks for me and personal entertainment. Amen.

Zimri, King of Israel

When a new regime takes over, they don't just depose the previous leader. All his relatives, friends, and supporters must be removed from office as well. Zimri made sure Baasha's family would not interfere with his reign.

After assassinating King Elah, Zimri reigned seven days in Israel in 885 BC. He committed suicide.

When [Zimri] became king, as soon as he was seated on his throne, Zimri struck down the entire house of Baasha. He did not leave a single male, including his kinsmen and his friends. So Zimri destroyed the entire house of Baasha, according to the word of the Lord he had spoken against Baasha through the prophet Jehu. This happened because of all the sins of Baasha and those of his son Elah, which they committed and caused Israel to commit, angering the Lord God of Israel with their worthless idols.

1 Kings 16:11–13 (CSB)

King Zimri murdered all of the family and friends of the former king's dynasty, so they would not challenge his reign. Zimri was an evil king even though he fulfilled the Lord's condemnation of Baasha's dynasty.

Because a new boss at the office is afraid of disloyal workers, those who supported the previous boss sometimes lose their jobs too. That is the world's way.

> Submit to every human authority because of the Lord, whether to the emperor as the supreme authority or to governors as those sent out by him to punish those who do what is evil and to praise those who do what is good.
>
> 1 Peter 2:13–14 (CSB)

I will respect whoever the new boss is. Even though I may not like office politics, I must honor all the leaders who are over me.

> PRAYER: Lord, help me give respect to my boss, in spite of office politics. Amen.

4

The era of Omri's dynasty (885–841 BC)

God's prophets were active throughout the time of the house divided. Elijah and his successor Elisha are among the most famous. Many of the prophetic books of the Old Testament were written while the house was divided. God's prophets were consistent voices against the idolatry and corruption of Israel and Judah. Kings were confronted for their sin and comforted when facing enemies.

This chapter includes devotional meditations on the following: Omri, King of Israel, and his descendants; kings of Judah who began their reigns during this time; the prophets Elijah and Elisha; and several others. This era ended when Joram of Israel and Ahaziah of Judah were killed.

Omri, King of Israel

The American Civil War (1861–1865) pitted those in the South who favored slavery against those opposed in the northern states. Several of my ancestors were Union soldiers in the Civil War. One was wounded and spent most of the war hospitalized. One barely survived in a prison camp. Another was a medic. In the end, slavery was abolished. Omri came to power after a civil war.

Omri did more evil than any of the previous kings of Israel.

He continued Jeroboam's idolatry in every respect. Omri reigned in Israel from about 885 to 874 BC.

> [When Zimri became king,] the troops were encamped against Gibbethon of the Philistines. When these troops heard that Zimri had not only conspired but had also struck down the king [Elah], then all Israel made Omri, the army commander, king over Israel that very day in the camp. Omri along with all Israel marched up from Gibbethon and besieged Tirzah. When Zimri saw that the city was captured, he entered the citadel of the royal palace and burned it down over himself…
>
> At that time the people of Israel were divided: half the people followed Tibni son of Ginath, to make him king, and half followed Omri. However, the people who followed Omri proved stronger than those who followed Tibni son of Ginath. So Tibni died and Omri became king.
>
> 1 Kings 16:15–22 (CSB)

Omri was named king of Israel by the army when they found out that Zimri had assassinated King Elah. When Omri's army captured the capital city Tirzah, Zimri committed suicide. Omri eventually won the civil war that followed.

Sometimes office politics degenerates into civil war, each side gathering an army. For example, I was in an ugly church business meeting. It seemed like an army was accusing the pastor. In the end, the congregation supported the pastor and the other side went to a different church.

> What is the source of wars and fights among you? Don't they come from your passions that wage war within you? You desire and do not have. You murder and covet and cannot obtain. You fight and wage war. You do not have because you do not ask. You ask and don't receive because you ask with wrong motives, so that you may spend it on your pleasures.
>
> James 4:1–3 (CSB)

James tells us the sources of such conflicts are selfish desires and corrupt motives. Believers are called to be peacemakers.

PRAYER: Lord, give me the grace to avoid civil wars. Amen.

Ahab, son of Omri, King of Israel

The First Lady of the United States is the wife of the President. She typically has ceremonial duties and often supports projects related to her public-policy interests. Ahab's First Lady introduced worship of Baal in Israel.

When his father died, Ahab became king. Ahab reigned in Israel from about 874 to 853 BC. He died in battle.

> As if following the sin of Jeroboam son of Nebat were not enough, [King Ahab] married Jezebel, the daughter of Ethbaal king of the Sidonians, and then proceeded to serve Baal and bow in worship to him. He set up an altar for Baal in the temple of Baal that he had built in Samaria. Ahab also made an Asherah pole. Ahab did more to anger the Lord God of Israel than all the kings of Israel who were before him.
>
> 1 Kings 16:31–33 (CSB)

Ahab married Jezebel, a pagan princess from Phoenicia. Due to her influence, he began to worship her god Baal. He built a temple and altar for Baal worship in his capital city Samaria and spread Baal worship throughout his kingdom. He was more evil than any of the kings of Israel before him.

When a believer's spouse is not a Christian, it is easy to fall into the spouse's worldly lifestyle and to adopt the spouse's priorities. Paul warned about partnering with unbelievers.

> Do not be yoked together with those who do not believe. For what partnership is there between righteousness and lawlessness? Or what fellowship does light have with darkness?
>
> 2 Corinthians 6:14 (CSB)

Sometimes the marriage ends when they cannot agree. It is important for both husband and wife to begin their marriage committed to the Lord.

PRAYER: Lord, thank you for a wife who loves you like I do. Amen.

Ahab and Naboth

Naboth had a vineyard near Ahab's palace in Jezreel. Ahab tried to buy the property, but Naboth refused because it was a family inheritance.

> But Naboth said to Ahab, "As the Lord is my witness, I will never give my ancestors' inheritance to you."
>
> So Ahab went to his palace resentful and angry because of what Naboth the Jezreelite had told him. He had said, "I will not give you my ancestors' inheritance." He lay down on his bed, turned his face away, and didn't eat any food...
>
> His wife Jezebel said to him, "Now, exercise your royal power over Israel. Get up, eat some food, and be happy. For I will give you the vineyard of Naboth the Jezreelite." ...
>
> When Ahab heard that Naboth was dead, he got up to go down to the vineyard of Naboth the Jezreelite to take possession of it.
>
> Then the word of the Lord came to Elijah the Tishbite: "Get up and go to meet King Ahab of Israel, who is in Samaria. He's in Naboth's vineyard, where he has gone to take possession of it. Tell him, 'This is what the Lord says: Have you murdered and also taken possession?' " ...
>
> Then the word of the Lord came to Elijah the Tishbite: "Have you seen how Ahab has humbled himself before me? I will not bring the disaster during his lifetime, because he has humbled himself before me. I

will bring the disaster on his house during his son's lifetime."

1 Kings 21:1–29 (CSB)

Ahab became depressed about Naboth's refusal, so his wife Jezebel arranged for the people of Jezreel to execute Naboth on a false charge. Ahab then took possession of the property.

The Lord sent the prophet Elijah to rebuke Ahab. He predicted Ahab's dynasty will be wiped out for all the evil Ahab had done. The king humbled himself, so the Lord relented and promised his dynasty will end in his son's reign instead of his own. However, Ahab did not repent of worshiping idols, and he kept Naboth's vineyard.

Disappointments can lead to depression like Ahab's. Sometimes the easy way out seems to be to manipulate people to do what I want, like Jezebel did. However, manipulation only produces bad results in the long run.

> Draw near to God, and he will draw near to you. Cleanse your hands, sinners, and purify your hearts, you double-minded. Be miserable and mourn and weep. Let your laughter be turned to mourning and your joy to gloom. Humble yourselves before the Lord, and he will exalt you.
>
> James 4:8–10 (CSB)

I was depressed when someone else in my department was promoted ahead of me. I told the Lord about my feelings and repented of my selfish motives. I asked him for help. I had to keep my hands off the situation and not complain. A humble attitude helped me get over the depression quickly. A year later, I started graduate school for the next chapter of my career. When I give my disappointments to the Lord and give him space to work, he produces good results. In the end, God's way works out best.

PRAYER: Lord, thank you for guiding the path of my career. Amen.

Widow of Zarephath

The news about the economy always has so many things to worry about: inflation, unemployment, debt, and so on. Trying to figure out what will happen in the world's economy only results in frustration, confusion, and headaches. Elijah prophesied that an economic disaster was coming.

After Elijah announced to Ahab there would be no rain, namely, a famine,[1] he hid at a creek near the Jordan river where ravens brought him food.

When the creek dried up, he went to Zarephath, which was a Phoenician town near Sidon, a pagan area.[2] When Elijah arrived at Zarephath, he met a widow, who was almost out of food due to the famine.

> [Elijah said to the widow,] "For this is what the Lord God of Israel says, 'The flour jar will not become empty and the oil jug will not run dry until the day the Lord sends rain on the surface of the land.' "
>
> So she proceeded to do according to the word of Elijah. Then the woman, Elijah, and her household ate for many days. The flour jar did not become empty, and the oil jug did not run dry, according to the word of the Lord he had spoken through Elijah.
>
> 1 Kings 17:14–16 (CSB)

Elijah told her if she would make him a small loaf with the flour and oil she had, the Lord promised that the flour and oil would last throughout the famine. Elijah obeyed the Lord by going to a pagan city. The widow obeyed the Lord by making a small loaf for Elijah. God was faithful through the three years of drought, and is faithful today.

> So don't worry, saying, 'What will we eat?' or 'What will we drink?' or 'What will we wear?' For the Gentiles eagerly seek all these things, and your heavenly

---

[1] 1 Kings 17:1–24.

[2] Zarephath was in modern Lebanon.

> Father knows that you need them. But seek first the
> kingdom of God and his righteousness, and all these
> things will be provided for you.
> Matthew 6:31–33 (CSB)

God has always provided what I needed when I obeyed his direction. For example, when I quit my job to go to graduate school full-time, our household income was cut by more than half. We didn't know how long our savings would last, paying for tuition. Shortly after school started, my wife got a big raise at her job. After a semester or two, I got a part time job at school teaching and later, doing research. God provided what we needed during those three years of school.

No matter what state the economy is in, or what my situation is, God's faithfulness is always there. God's direction leads to resources I didn't know about.

> PRAYER: Lord, thank you for your care for me and my
> family. Amen.

Elijah, prophet of the Lord

An athletic contest determines whose team is most powerful. American football teams have the loyalty of entire cities and regions. International football (soccer) national teams have the loyalty of entire nations. Which nation is most powerful? Elijah proposed a contest to see whose God is most powerful.

After about three years without rain, Elijah went to Ahab and proposed a contest between the Lord and the Baal.[3] All of Israel gathered at Mount Carmel to see the spectacle. There were 450 prophets of Baal against one prophet of the Lord, Elijah. Whichever god burned the sacrifice would be the winner.

The prophets of Baal prepared their sacrifice, but did not light the fire. They called all morning and into the afternoon, "Baal, answer us!" They shouted, danced, and cut themselves. There was no reply and no fire.

---

[3]1 Kings 17:1; 18:1–46.

Elijah prepared his stone altar, dug a trench around it, and arranged his sacrifice. He had servants drench the sacrifice and altar with water filling the trench. When he prayed, fire fell consuming the sacrifice and all the water.

The people exclaimed, "The Lord, he is God! The Lord, he is God!" At Elijah's direction, they executed the pagan prophets.

> Elijah said to Ahab, "Go up, eat and drink, for there is the sound of a rainstorm."
>
> So Ahab went to eat and drink, but Elijah went up to the summit of Carmel. He bent down on the ground and put his face between his knees. Then he said to his servant, "Go up and look toward the sea."
>
> So he went up, looked, and said, "There's nothing."
>
> Seven times Elijah said, "Go back."
>
> On the seventh time, he reported, "There's a cloud as small as a man's hand coming up from the sea."
>
> 1 Kings 18:41–44 (CSB)

After the victory over the prophets of Baal, Elijah went up Mount Carmel to pray alone. God had answered his proclamation of a drought. God had answered his prayer for fire from heaven. Now he was praying for rain to end the drought. Over and over, he sent his servant to look at the Mediterranean Sea for the answer. He kept praying until there was a small cloud. That was all the evidence he needed. He sent his servant to tell the king the rain was coming. The Lord was ending the drought.

James pointed out that Elijah was a human being just like we are, so we should pray earnestly like he did.

> The prayer of a righteous person is very powerful in its effect. Elijah was a human being as we are, and he prayed earnestly that it would not rain, and for three years and six months it did not rain on the land. Then he prayed again, and the sky gave rain and the land produced its fruit.
>
> James 5:16–18 (CSB)

34

God will answer like he did for Elijah. Sometimes persistent prayer is necessary. For example, my wife Angie's grandmother prayed daily for her and her mother to have saving relationships with Jesus. They eventually became whole hearted followers of Jesus. I am determined to pray persistently like Elijah. His experience illustrates God's faithfulness, even in difficult situations.

> PRAYER: Lord, thank you for your faithfulness in difficult situations. Amen.

Elijah at Mount Horeb

When Jezebel learned what had happened at Mount Carmel, she promised to kill Elijah. He ran for his life.[4] He left his servant in Beer-sheba, and proceeded alone into the desert. In despair, he prayed for death and then fell asleep under a tree. An angel woke him up with food and water to renew his strength, so he could walk to Mount Horeb, also called Mount Sinai, where he spent the night in a cave.

> Then [the Lord said to Elijah], "Go out and stand on the mountain in the Lord's presence."
>
> At that moment, the Lord passed by. A great and mighty wind was tearing at the mountains and was shattering cliffs before the Lord, but the Lord was not in the wind. After the wind there was an earthquake, but the Lord was not in the earthquake. After the earthquake there was a fire, but the Lord was not in the fire. And after the fire there was a voice, a soft whisper. When Elijah heard it, he wrapped his face in his mantle and went out and stood at the entrance of the cave.
>
> Suddenly, a voice came to him and said, "What are you doing here, Elijah?"
>
> 1 Kings 19:11–13 (CSB)

---

[4] 1 Kings 19:1–18.

The Lord confronted Elijah. Before he could emerge from the cave, there were dramatic signs of God's power: a violent wind, an earthquake, and fire. But the Lord was not present in them. When Elijah heard a whisper, he knew the Lord was there. So he covered his face with his mantle and came out of the cave, as God had demanded. The Lord has given the Holy Spirit to each believer today. Sometimes he whispers.

> Don't you know that your body is a temple of the Holy Spirit who is in you, whom you have from God? You are not your own.
>
> 1 Corinthians 6:19 (CSB)

The Holy Spirit speaks, moves, and empowers believers to become mature Christians. We belong to Christ.

Like Elijah, a whisper or a nudge is what I feel when the Holy Spirit speaks to me. The Lord doesn't announce his presence to me with dramatic signs of his power. He doesn't give me long explanations of what he wants. Just a word is enough. He is gentle. I have to be attentive, or I might miss him.

> PRAYER: Lord, thank you for speaking to me. I will try not to miss even a word. Amen.

Ben-hadad, King of Aram

Many people must think God lives in church buildings. That is the only place they look for him. Religious rituals are supposed to get his attention and earn his favor. King Ben-hadad too thought the Lord was just a local god.

Ben-hadad, King of Aram, and his allies assembled a huge army to attack Israel and besiege the capital, Samaria.[5] After futile negotiations with the enemy, a prophet of the Lord gave King Ahab a strategy that routed them. The prophet warned Ahab that the king of Aram would attack again the next year.

---

[5] 1 Kings 20:1–43.

> Now the king of Aram's servants said to him, "Their
> gods are gods of the hill country. That's why they
> were stronger than we were. Instead, we should fight
> with them on the plain; then we will certainly be
> stronger than they are."
>
> 1 Kings 20:23 (CSB)

After Aram's defeat, Ben-hadad's pagan advisers recommended forming another army to attack Israel. They claimed Israel's god was limited to the hills and that was why their army was defeated. The king was convinced, so they planned to fight on the plain.

The next year, the army of Aram took their positions near Aphek, and Israel's army arrayed against them. The army of Israel looked tiny compared to that of Aram. The prophet of the Lord told Ahab how Aram had insulted the Lord, so he predicted Israel would rout the army of Aram again, and they did. The Lord is master of the hills and master of the plain.

Ben-hadad thought the Lord stays in the hills. Many churchgoers today must think God stays in the church building. That is they only place they pray, and they don't expect him to intervene in their problems during the week. They are religious on Sundays, but they fight their battles by themselves on Monday.

> The God who made the world and everything in it—
> he is Lord of heaven and earth—does not live in
> shrines made by hands. Neither is he served by human hands, as though he needed anything, since he
> himself gives everyone life and breath and all things.
>
> Acts 17:24–25 (CSB)

Of course, God is not limited to church buildings. I can and should pray to him anytime and anywhere. He is eager to demonstrate his love for me through my circumstances. I don't have to fight my battles alone.[6] The Lord is there to help me.

PRAYER: Lord, thank you for being with me in the middle of my battles. Amen.

---

[6]Romans 8:35–39.

Jehoshaphat, son of Asa, King of Judah

Who do you go to for good advice? Some people ask their friends. Some look on the Internet. Some try to find an expert, a professional. King Jehoshaphat wanted advice from the Lord.

Jehoshaphat reigned in Judah from about 872 to 847 BC. He followed the Lord like his father Asa.[7]

King Jehoshaphat of Judah was allied with King Ahab of Israel. Before they went into battle together, Jehoshaphat insisted they get advice from a prophet of the Lord.

> But Jehoshaphat asked [Ahab, King of Israel], "Isn't there a prophet of the Lord here anymore? Let's ask him."
>
> The king of Israel said to Jehoshaphat, "There is still one man who can inquire of the Lord, but I hate him because he never prophesies good about me, but only disaster. He is Micaiah son of Imlah."
>
> 1 Kings 22:7–8 (CSB)

Another time, King Jehoshaphat of Judah was allied with King Joram of Israel, who was the son of Ahab. Again, before they went into battle together, Jehoshaphat insisted they get advice from a prophet of the Lord.

> But Jehoshaphat said [to Joram, King of Israel], "Isn't there a prophet of the Lord here? Let's inquire of the Lord through him."
>
> One of the servants of the king of Israel answered, "Elisha son of Shaphat, who used to pour water on Elijah's hands, is here."
>
> Jehoshaphat affirmed, "The word of the Lord is with him." So the king of Israel and Jehoshaphat and the king of Edom went to him.
>
> 2 Kings 3:11–12 (CSB)

---

[7]1 Kings 22:43–46.

The kings of Israel almost never asked for advice from a prophet of the Lord, but Jehoshaphat did.

In the New Testament we also see examples of believers seeking advice from the Lord.

> When [Paul and his companions] came to Mysia, they tried to go into Bithynia, but the Spirit of Jesus did not allow them. Passing by Mysia they went down to [the city of] Troas.
>
> Acts 16:7–8 (CSB)

Paul sought guidance from the Lord as they traveled. They had preached throughout the region of Phrygia, but the Holy Spirit did not allow them to preach in the regions of Asia, Mysia, or Bithynia. This prepared them to go to Macedonia.

Whenever I'm working on a project, I should follow Jehoshaphat's example, praying for the Lord's advice.

> PRAYER: Lord, I always need your advice, no matter what I'm working on. Amen.

Ahaziah, son of Ahab, King of Israel

When I get injured in an accident, I want to know if I'll fully recover. Medical science knows some things. A doctor will tell me how most people respond to treatment, but the doctor can't be sure what will happen to me. Ahaziah wanted to know if he would recover from an accidental fall.

Ahaziah reigned in Israel less than two years from about 853 to 852 BC.

> [King] Ahaziah had fallen through the latticed window of his upstairs room in Samaria and was injured. So he sent messengers, instructing them, "Go inquire of Baal-zebub, the god of Ekron, whether I will recover from this injury."
>
> But the angel of the Lord said to Elijah the Tishbite, "Go and meet the messengers of the king of Samaria."
> . . .

Ahaziah died according to the word of the Lord that Elijah had spoken.

2 Kings 1:2–17 (CSB)

King Ahaziah was injured by a fall through an upper floor window. He sent messengers to the Philistine city of Ekron to get a prognosis. The prophet Elijah intercepted the messengers and reproved the king for seeking a word from a pagan idol instead from the Lord. Elijah predicted the king would die of his injuries.

When a problem in life pops up, worldly sources are always available. The latest popular fad will heal every ache or pain, so they say. Doctors can give me a prognosis based on medical science.

To one is given a message of wisdom through the Spirit, to another, a message of knowledge by the same Spirit.

1 Corinthians 12:8 (CSB)

Words of wisdom and knowledge are gifts from the Holy Spirit. Prayer is my first step. The Holy Spirit guides me to the true information I need to know and the helpers he has prepared for me. The Lord knows the outcome from the beginning.

PRAYER: Lord, when a problem in life pops up, I will go to you first. Amen.

Elisha called

Career changes can be intimidating. Suppose I have to replace my boss who is retiring. My thoughts would race ahead. "I was comfortable in my old job. Will I like the new job? Will I be able to do a good job like he does?" Elijah was the most famous prophet to Israel. Who could possibly take his place?

While Elijah was at Mount Horeb, the Lord told him who was to be his successor as prophet to Israel,[8] so he went to look for Elisha.

---

[8] 1 Kings 19:16.

Elijah left [Horeb] and found Elisha son of Shaphat as he was plowing. Twelve teams of oxen were in front of him, and he was with the twelfth team. Elijah walked by him and threw his mantle over him. Elisha left the oxen, ran to follow Elijah, and said, "Please let me kiss my father and mother, and then I will follow you."

"Go on back," he replied, "for what have I done to you?"

So he turned back from following him, took the team of oxen, and slaughtered them. With the oxen's wooden yoke and plow, he cooked the meat and gave it to the people, and they ate. Then he left, followed Elijah, and served him.

1 Kings 19:19–21 (CSB)

Elijah found Elisha working on his farm. Elijah's mantle on Elisha indicated the call to follow. Elisha responded by slaughtering his oxen and burning the farm implements for a feast. The whole community saw he could never go back to farming. Elijah did not have a servant, so Elisha became his servant.

Elisha was faced with a career change. Would he leave farming to become a prophet of the Lord? Elijah was obviously the best possible mentor. It meant leaving home and never returning to farming. Elisha gladly obeyed the call.

Jesus called Simon Peter, Andrew, James, and John to leave their jobs as fishermen to follow him. It meant more than a career change.

As he passed alongside the Sea of Galilee, he saw Simon and Andrew, Simon's brother, casting a net into the sea—for they were fishermen. "Follow me," Jesus told them, "and I will make you fish for people." Immediately they left their nets and followed him. Going on a little farther, he saw James the son of Zebedee and his brother John in a boat putting their nets in order. Immediately he called them, and they left their father Zebedee in the boat with the hired men and followed him.

Mark 1:16–20 (CSB)

41

Every time I've changed jobs, it meant more than a career change, because I am following Jesus. After twenty years in a career developing software, I felt the call to become a teacher at a university. With my wife's support, I quit my job and enrolled to get the necessary ticket, a Ph.D. My adviser was my mentor in computer-science research. A career change felt intimidating, but when God confirmed the call, I knew it was the right direction.

PRAYER: Lord, thank you for your guidance and confirmations as I faced changes. Amen.

Elisha, prophet of the Lord

Elijah apparently knew when his time was almost over. Elijah and Elisha traveled through Gilgal, Bethel, and Jericho to the Jordan River. At each stop, Elijah challenged Elisha to stay behind, but Elisha would not leave his master. He was committed to becoming a prophet of the Lord. In Bethel and Jericho, there were communities of prophets who predicted Elijah would be taken, but Elisha persevered.

> Elijah took his mantle, rolled it up, and struck the water [of the Jordan River], which parted to the right and left. Then the two of them crossed over on dry ground. When they had crossed over, Elijah said to Elisha, "Tell me what I can do for you before I am taken from you."
>
> So Elisha answered, "Please, let me inherit two shares of your spirit."
>
> Elijah replied, "You have asked for something difficult. If you see me being taken from you, you will have it. If not, you won't."
>
> As they continued walking and talking, a chariot of fire with horses of fire suddenly appeared and separated the two of them. Then Elijah went up into heaven in the whirlwind. As Elisha watched, he kept crying out, "My father, my father, the chariots and horsemen of Israel!"

42

When he could see him no longer, he took hold of his own clothes, tore them in two, picked up the mantle that had fallen off Elijah, and went back and stood on the bank of the Jordan. He took the mantle Elijah had dropped, and he struck the water. "Where is the Lord God of Elijah?" he asked. He struck the water himself, and it parted to the right and the left, and Elisha crossed over.

2 Kings 2:8–14 (CSB)

The Jordan River was impassable, so Elijah miraculously parted the water and they crossed to the east side. Elisha knew he would become the leading prophet to Israel, so he asked for a double inheritance of Elijah's spirit. This was obviously in the Lord's hands. As they continued, a fiery chariot in a tornado took Elijah.

As they traveled, Elisha knew he was going to lose his mentor. He probably wondered if he could be an effective prophet to Israel. When Elisha returned to the Jordan River, he parted the water like Elijah had done. The Lord confirmed his new role.

When Jesus ascended into heaven, Peter, Andrew, James, John, and the other disciples didn't know what lay ahead. They had their instructions, so they waited. Then Pentecost arrived.

While [Jesus] was with [the disciples], he commanded them not to leave Jerusalem, but to wait for the Father's promise. "Which," he said, "you have heard me speak about; for John baptized with water, but you will be baptized with the Holy Spirit in a few days."

Acts 1:4–5 (CSB)

After graduation, I didn't know what lay ahead. I continued working as a researcher for five years. My wife and I continued to serve in our church. When the time came to apply for a job a thousand miles away, I knew it meant leaving my professional mentor and the leaders of my church. I didn't know what kind of service to the Lord was ahead. During the interview process, the Lord confirmed we were going in the right direction. He separately gave my wife and I assurance.

PRAYER: Lord, thank you for your peace as my wife and I submit our decisions to you. Amen.

Widow of a prophet

Many people these days live from one paycheck to the next. Suddenly, there is a financial crisis when an unexpected expense arises or their job goes away. In ancient Israel, a widow would be desperate, because there was no longer a husband to provide for the family.

In Elisha's time, there were communities of prophets of the Lord in various places, called "sons of the prophets." A destitute widow of a prophet appealed to Elisha because creditors were threatening to enslave her children.[9] All she had was a jar of oil. Elisha told her to borrow as many containers as she could from neighbors.

> After she had shut the door behind her and her sons, they kept bringing her containers, and she kept pouring. When they were full, she said to her son, "Bring me another container."
>
> But he replied, "There aren't any more." Then the oil stopped.
>
> She went and told the man of God, and he said, "Go sell the oil and pay your debt; you and your sons can live on the rest."
>
> 2 Kings 4:5–7 (CSB)

The widow's small jar of oil was miraculously poured out into many large containers. She had faith in God to do what the prophet said. God provided enough to meet her need.

> And my God will supply all your needs according to his riches in glory in Christ Jesus.
>
> Philippians 4:19 (CSB)

---

[9] 2 Kings 4:1–7.

While I was a student and our household finances were limited, my wife and I received an invitation to go to Malaysia from a missionary friend there. Our hearts said "Yes!" even though we didn't have money for the trip. We made travel plans and reservations anyway about six months in advance. A few months before the trip, we received enough to pay for the trip from an unexpected source. The trip was a wonderful experience serving the Christians there. God provides when we are following his plan.

> PRAYER: Lord, thank you for providing the money we needed to follow your plan. Amen.

Naaman, commander of Aram

When a high government official gets sick, the very best doctors are mobilized. The official may even go to another country to find better medical care. If it is an incurable disease, he will still hope for a miracle drug. Naaman was such an official.

Naaman was commander of the army of Aram, a pagan.[10] He had a skin disease. A slave girl from Israel in his household said the prophet Elisha could cure him. So the king of Aram sent Naaman to the capital of Israel with a letter and a huge gift, asking the king of Israel to heal Naaman. Knowing that such healing was humanly impossible, the king of Israel thought this was a diplomatic plot to start a war. When Elisha heard about this, he asked for Naaman to come to him, so Naaman came to Elisha's door.

> Then Elisha sent [Naaman] a messenger, who said, "Go wash seven times in the Jordan and your skin will be restored and you will be clean."
>
> But Naaman got angry and left, saying, "I was telling myself: He will surely come out, stand and call on the name of the Lord his God, and wave his hand over the place and cure the skin disease. Aren't Abana and Pharpar, the rivers of Damascus, better than all

---

[10]2 Kings 5:1–27.

the waters of Israel? Couldn't I wash in them and be clean?" So he turned and left in a rage.

But his servants approached and said to him, "My father, if the prophet had told you to do some great thing, would you not have done it? How much more should you do it when he only tells you, 'Wash and be clean'?"

So Naaman went down and dipped himself in the Jordan seven times, according to the command of the man of God. Then his skin was restored and became like the skin of a small boy, and he was clean.

2 Kings 5:10–14 (CSB)

Elisha told Naaman to do a simple act of faith to be healed, namely, to dip seven times in the Jordan River. Naaman was offended. He expected a big religious ceremony that was suitable for his rank. He despised the Jordan River. However, his servants persuaded him to try it because the required task was so simple. When he dipped in the water, as Elisha had said, he was healed.

Naaman had learned that the Lord is the only true God. He promised to worship only the Lord God of Israel. But he received permission to go into pagan temples as part of his job.

In the same way, Jesus looked for simple faith expressed by simple actions. For example, he put mud on the eyes of a man born blind.

As long as I am in the world, I am the light of the world." After he said these things he spit on the ground, made some mud from the saliva, and spread the mud on his eyes. "Go," he told him, "wash in the pool of Siloam" (which means "Sent"). So he left, washed, and came back seeing.

John 9:5–7 (CSB)

The Lord doesn't care about a person's rank. He doesn't care about big religious ceremonies. The Lord is looking for obedience based on faith.

PRAYER: Lord, my faith seems small. I just want to obey you. Amen.

Servant of Elisha

A spy for the enemy will try to find out the army's secrets. If it seems the enemy knows about the army's plans, then they must capture the spy.

The king of Aram was frustrated because the Lord kept revealing to Elisha what the army of Aram was doing, and Elisha kept reporting this to the king of Israel.[11] So, the king of Aram sent an army to capture Elisha. They surrounded Elisha's city at night.

> When the servant of the man of God got up early and went out, he discovered an army [of Aram] with horses and chariots surrounding the city. So he asked Elisha, "Oh, my master, what are we to do?"
>
> Elisha said, "Don't be afraid, for those who are with us outnumber those who are with them."
>
> Then Elisha prayed, "Lord, please open his eyes and let him see." So the Lord opened the servant's eyes, and he saw that the mountain was covered with horses and chariots of fire all around Elisha.
>
> 2 Kings 6:15–17 (CSB)

Elisha's servant saw the army of Aram all around their city. The situation looked hopeless. Elisha told him not to worry. He prayed for his servant's eyes to be opened. Then the servant saw God's army of fire on the mountain behind the army of Aram.

The Lord struck the army of Aram with blindness. Elisha then delivered them to the king of Israel, who fed them and sent them home.

> Don't neglect to show hospitality, for by doing this some have welcomed angels as guests without knowing it.
>
> Hebrews 13:2 (CSB)

---

[11]2 Kings 6:8–23.

Angie was alone at home one afternoon. She sang some Scripture choruses as she played her guitar. Then she noticed in her peripheral vision an angel standing across the room. He was about nine feet tall, almost to the ceiling, dressed in white. Awestruck, she just kept playing and singing. She supposed he liked worship. After he was gone, like Elisha's servant, she knew an angel was nearby.

PRAYER: Lord, make me sensitive to perceive your presence and the presence of your messengers. Amen.

Hazael, King of Aram

When the head of a country becomes sick, everyone wants to know the prognosis. Will he die? If he dies, who will take over? There are so many questions. The Lord sent Elisha to anoint the next king of Aram.

Elisha went to the capital of Aram when the pagan king was sick.[12] The king sent Hazael, one of his officials, to Elisha to find out if he would recover. Elisha said to Hazael, "Go say to him, 'You are sure to recover.' But the Lord has shown me that he is sure to die."

> The man of God wept, and Hazael asked, "Why is my lord weeping?"
>
> He replied, "Because I know the evil you will do to the people of Israel. You will set their fortresses on fire. You will kill their young men with the sword. You will dash their children to pieces. You will rip open their pregnant women."
>
> Hazael said, "How could your servant, a mere dog, do such a mighty deed?"
>
> Elisha answered, "The Lord has shown me that you will be king over Aram."
>
> 2 Kings 8:11–13 (CSB)

[12] 2 Kings 8:7–15.

48

Elisha was there to anoint Hazael as king over Aram. Elisha wept because he knew in future wars Hazael would do terrible things to Israel.

The next day Hazael murdered the king, smothering him with a wet cloth, and then became king himself. Perhaps Hazael was planning to do this all along. Elisha proved the Lord knew the secrets of Hazael's heart. The Lord sees the secret plots and schemes of men.

Jesus warned us that conditions in the world will become worse and worse, but we are secure in his love.

> You are going to hear of wars and rumors of wars. See that you are not alarmed, because these things must take place, but the end is not yet.
>
> Matthew 24:6 (CSB)

When I read the news with eyes of faith, plots and schemes are often obvious. Knowing God's standards of truth, righteousness, and justice let's me recognize and anticipate the consequences of sin. I mourn when sin seems overwhelming. It makes me happy when I read about acts of kindness and godly righteousness.

> PRAYER: Lord, give me your eyes to understand the righteousness and sin happening in the world. Amen.

Jehoram, son of Jehoshaphat, King of Judah

When two kings were political allies, sometimes a prince from one country would marry a princess from the other. This would strengthen their alliance. Jehoshaphat of Judah was an ally of Israel, so his son married a princess of Israel. Maybe he liked her too.

Jehoram reigned in Judah from about 852 to 841 BC. He was coregent with his father for a few years.[13]

---

[13]2 Kings 8:16–24.

[King Jehoram] walked in the ways of the kings of Israel, as the house of Ahab had done, for Ahab's daughter [Athaliah] was his wife. He did what was evil in the Lord's sight.

2 Kings 8:18 (CSB)

King Jehoram of Judah married King Ahab's daughter from Israel. Due to her influence, he worshiped Baal and other idols like the kings of Israel, instead of worshiping the Lord like his father. The result was tragic for Judah.

This same dynamic is experienced by modern couples when one spouse has a church-going background, but the other spouse wants a middle class lifestyle with all its status symbols. After a while, they both become focused on materialism. The outcome can be tragic.

Flee from youthful passions, and pursue righteousness, faith, love, and peace, along with those who call on the Lord from a pure heart.

2 Timothy 2:22 (CSB)

A successful marriage is founded on both husband and wife worshiping the Lord from the heart.

PRAYER: Lord, thank you for a successful marriage. Give me the words I need to counsel others. Amen.

Joram, son of Ahab, King of Israel

In America, the Democratic party and the Republican party jockey to rule the nation. Whenever there is a political change, some policies are changed and some stay the same. When Joram became king, he changed the religion policy in Israel.

Joram reigned in Israel from about 852 to 841 BC. He was also called Jehoram. Ahaziah had no son, so his brother Joram succeeded him as king. He was killed by Jehu.[14]

---

[14]2 Kings 3:1–3.

> [King Joram] did what was evil in the Lord's sight, but not like his father [Ahab] and mother [Jezebel], for he removed the sacred pillar of Baal his father had made.
>
> 2 Kings 3:2 (CSB)

King Joram continued worship of the gold calves and other idols that had long been worshiped in Israel. Even though he deemphasized worship of Baal, he still was an evil king.

Deemphasizing one idol in favor of traditional idols is still not pleasing to the Lord.

> I say this and testify in the Lord: You should no longer walk as the Gentiles do, in the futility of their thoughts... They became callous and gave themselves over to promiscuity for the practice of every kind of impurity with a desire for more and more.
>
> Ephesians 4:17–19 (CSB)

A local businessman at my church made a large pledge to the building fund. He understood the Bible teaches us to be generous. However, he continued to live with his girlfriend and promoted a get-rich-quick scheme. There are many things people do today which are traditional idols in our culture. There are no excuses for pursuing them.

> PRAYER: Lord, give me your insight into the traditions of society today. Amen.

Ahaziah, son of Jehoram, King of Judah

A young man often continues to worship the same way his parents did, especially while they are still alive. Ahaziah's mother was very influential during his reign.

Ahaziah reigned in Judah less than a year in about 841 BC. He was named for his uncle, Ahaziah, King of Israel. He was killed by Jehu's men.

[King Ahaziah] walked in the ways of the house of Ahab and did what was evil in the Lord's sight like the house of Ahab, for his father had married into the house of Ahab.

2 Kings 8:27 (CSB)

King Ahaziah was twenty-two years old when he became king of Judah. During his short reign, he continued to worship Baal and other idols like his father due to the influence of his mother Athaliah who was a daughter of Ahab, King of Israel.

Children often subconsciously inherit life patterns from their parents. For example, Paul commended the faith of Timothy's mother and grandmother.

I recall your sincere faith that first lived in your grandmother Lois and in your mother Eunice and now, I am convinced, is in you also.

2 Timothy 1:5 (CSB)

I was influenced in a positive way by my mother's faith in Jesus. She made sure I was taught what the Bible says. By the time I was twenty-two, like Ahaziah, I was secure in my own faith.

PRAYER: Lord, thank you for the good example of my mother's faith. Amen.

5

The era of Jehu's dynasty (841–753 BC)

Baal was one of the gods worshiped by the Phoenicians.[1] Ahab's wife Jezebel introduced Baal worship in Israel. Ahab's daughter Athaliah married Jehoram, King of Judah. She introduced Baal worship in Judah. Getting rid of Baal worship took radical action by Jehu in Israel and Joash in Judah.

This chapter includes devotional meditations on the following: Jehu, King of Israel, and his descendants; the kings of Judah who began their reigns during this time; and some workmen. This era ended when the fourth generation of Jehu's descendants was assassinated, fulfilling a prophecy given to Jehu.

Jehu, son of Jehoshaphat, King of Israel

Throughout church history there have been religious crusaders and popular movements. They often challenged the established church leadership, attacked corruption, argued over theology, and changed traditional practices. Jehu was a religious crusader.

Jehu reigned in Israel from about 841 to 814 BC.[2]

---

[1]Phoenicia was in modern Lebanon.

[2]2 Kings 9:1–10:36. Jehu was not the son of Jehoshaphat, King of Judah. He was son of another Jehoshaphat, son of Nimshi.

Elisha sent one of the prophets to anoint Jehu as king of Israel. Jehu was army commander at that time and the army officers supported him becoming king. Jehu murdered Joram, King of Israel, and his men murdered Ahaziah, King of Judah, who was visiting Joram at that time. Jehu then became King of Israel.

Jehu executed all of Ahab's male descendants, officials, and friends. He also executed Jezebel, the queen mother, who financially supported the priests of Baal. In a deceptive plan, he gathered all the servants of Baal into the idol's temple in the capital city, Samaria. When he gave the signal, his men killed them all.

> So [Jehu's men] struck [all the servants of Baal] down with the sword. Then the guards and officers threw the bodies out and went into the inner room of the temple of Baal. They brought out the pillar of the temple of Baal and burned it, and they tore down the pillar of Baal. Then they tore down the temple of Baal and made it a latrine—which it still is today. Jehu eliminated Baal worship from Israel.
>
> 2 Kings 10:25–28 (CSB)

After killing all the servants of Baal, Jehu's men tore down the Baal idol and burned it. They tore down the temple of Baal and made it a latrine for sewage. Even though Jehu eliminated Baal worship in Israel, the people continued to worship the gold calves and other idols set up by Jeroboam.

A religious crusader often focuses on getting rid of one kind of sin in the church. Sermons, videos, and conferences push the message of repentance from that sin. However, such a movement often overlooks other sins entangling people.

For example, a famous evangelist preached one Sunday in my church. The next Sunday, my pastor had to correct what the evangelist had said. The evangelist's message was unbalanced.

> Be diligent to present yourself to God as one approved, a worker who doesn't need to be ashamed, correctly teaching the word of truth.
>
> 2 Timothy 2:15 (CSB)

A balanced understanding of the whole Bible equips me to properly evaluate religious crusaders and other famous Bible teachers. Balance is also necessary when applying the Bible to my life.

> PRAYER: Lord, give me a balanced understanding of the Bible. Show me what is important. Amen.

Athaliah, mother of Ahaziah, Queen of Judah

When a founding pastor retires, finding his successor is often awkward. Sometimes it becomes a political battle. An ambitious relative of the former pastor may want the position. Athaliah held the important office of queen mother. She was an ambitious usurper.

Athaliah reigned in Judah from about 841 to 835 BC.[3] Athaliah was executed when Joash became king.

> When Athaliah, Ahaziah's mother, saw that her son was dead, she proceeded to annihilate all the royal heirs. Jehosheba, who was King Jehoram's daughter and Ahaziah's sister, secretly rescued Joash son of Ahaziah from among the king's sons who were being killed and put him and the one who nursed him in a bedroom. So he was hidden from Athaliah and was not killed. Joash was in hiding with her in the Lord's temple six years while Athaliah reigned over the land.
>
> 2 Kings 11:1–3 (CSB)

Instead of supporting the coronation of one of her grandsons, Athaliah murdered them and seized the throne for herself. However, Ahaziah's sister rescued her nephew Joash who was about one year old. During her reign, Athaliah continued worship of

---

[3]2 Kings 11:1–16.

Baal in Judah which she had imported from Israel. She was following in Jezebel's footsteps, corrupting the people of Judah.

Corrupt leaders can damage the faith of church members. Jesus reproved the church in Thyatira because they tolerated evil leadership.[4]

> But I have this against you: You tolerate the woman Jezebel, who calls herself a prophetess and teaches and deceives my servants to commit sexual immorality and to eat meat sacrificed to idols.
>
> Revelation 2:20 (CSB)

Thyatira had a prophetess Jesus called "Jezebel," because she was corrupting the church like the wife of King Ahab did to Israel. Jesus promised to judge her and her friends in Thyatira. Jesus advised those who were not following her to hold on to what is good.

From time to time, we hear of scandals where church leaders fall into sin. Sometime they even refuse to admit there is a moral problem. Naturally, followers are disappointed when the truth is revealed. My faith is not damaged by someone else's sin. I will hold on to what is good, even if local leaders are corrupt.

> PRAYER: Lord, I may grieve over corrupt leaders and their mistakes, but my faith is in you. Amen.

Joash, son of Ahaziah, King of Judah

When a young person is promoted to position of authority, he needs mentors and staff who will wisely guide him. Joash was a very young king.

Joash reigned in Judah from about 835 to 796 BC.[5] He was assassinated.

> Joash was seven years old when he became king. In the seventh year of Jehu, Joash became king, and he

---

[4]Revelation 2:18–29.
[5]2 Kings 11:1–12:21.

reigned forty years in Jerusalem. His mother's name was Zibiah; she was from Beer-sheba. Throughout the time the priest Jehoiada instructed him, Joash did what was right in the Lord's sight.

2 Kings 11:21; 12:1–2 (CSB)

At the time of Joash's coronation, the priest Jehoiada renewed the people's covenant with the Lord and then the people eliminated Baal worship from Judah. In Joash's early years, Jehoiada was his mentor. However, the people continued to worship idols at the high places.

Paul encouraged Timothy to mentor reliable men in his church.

What you have heard from me in the presence of many witnesses, commit to faithful men who will be able to teach others also.

2 Timothy 2:2 (CSB)

When I look back on my teen years, I appreciate the men who taught me the Bible in Sunday School and the director of the youth group who taught me about good relationships. A godly mentor helps a young person develop faith and good patterns in life.

PRAYER: Lord, thank you for the mentors you sent to me. Help me be a good mentor to others. Amen.

Supervisors of workmen in the temple

Every church needs people who will handle the finances honestly. Misuse of church money is the root of many church scandals. Joash found the honest helpers he needed.

After many years of idol worship in Judah, the Lord's temple had deteriorated. During his reign, King Joash ordered the temple be repaired.[6] The priests did not follow through on his orders, so he appointed supervisors and workmen to do the repairs and made financial arrangements.

---

[6]2 Kings 12:4–16.

[The king's secretary and the high priest] would give the weighed silver to those doing the work—those who oversaw the Lord's temple. They in turn would pay it out to those working on the Lord's temple— the carpenters, the builders, the masons, and the stonecutters—and would use it to buy timber and quarried stone to repair the damage to the Lord's temple and for all expenses for temple repairs... [The silver] was given to those doing the work, and they repaired the Lord's temple with it. No accounting was required from the men who received the silver to pay those doing the work, since they worked with integrity.

2 Kings 12:11–15 (CSB)

Silver offerings were collected at the temple gate from the people. Instead of making implements for temple use, the silver was tallied and given to supervisors who disbursed it to the workers. The supervisors were commended for their integrity. They were trusted without requiring an accounting.

Men of integrity were also important in New Testament churches. Paul made sure the Greek Christians' offering for relief in Judea was safeguarded with integrity.

We have sent with [Titus] the brother who is praised among all the churches for his gospel ministry. And not only that, but he was also appointed by the churches to accompany us with this gracious gift that we are administering for the glory of the Lord himself and to show our eagerness to help. We are taking this precaution so that no one will criticize us about this large sum that we are administering.

2 Corinthians 8:18–20 (CSB)

Churches today usually have traditional accounting and bookkeeping safeguards, so the world cannot accuse the church of corruption. Sometime a small church will trust just a few members with all the financial details which leaves them vulnerable to abuse. Many Christian nonprofit organizations belong to the Evangelical Council for Financial Accountability (ECFA) and follow their recommended practices.

> PRAYER: Lord, thank you for those in my church who serve, handling the finances with integrity. Amen.

Jehoahaz, son of Jehu, King of Israel

When I have a crisis, who can I go to for help? Friends and relatives have limited resources. Government programs have too much red tape. Maybe prayer will help. Jehoahaz had a crisis. Aram had demolished his army.

Jehoahaz reigned in Israel from about 814 to 798 BC.[7] Due to the continued idolatry of Israel, the Lord allowed Hazael, king of Aram, and his son Ben-hadad to oppress Israel.

> Jehoahaz sought the Lord's favor, and the Lord heard him, for he saw the oppression the king of Aram inflicted on Israel. Therefore, the Lord gave Israel a deliverer, and they escaped from the power of the Arameans.
>
> 2 Kings 13:4–5 (CSB)

King Jehoahaz continued worship of the gold calves set up by Jeroboam, the Ashera poles, and other idols. But when Aram destroyed Israel's army and oppressed Israel, Jehoahaz sought help from the Lord, instead of the idols. The Lord provided a deliverer, so the oppression by Aram stopped. However, the people returned to their former way of life, worshiping idols.

Jesus promised us peace even in the middle of hardship.

> I have told you these things so that in me you may have peace. You will have suffering in this world. Be courageous! I have conquered the world.
>
> John 16:33 (CSB)

---

[7] 2 Kings 13:1–9.

When a crisis comes, a worldly person may remember how he prayed to the Lord as a child. If he will turn to the Lord, God will provide his solution to the crisis. The Lord loves his rebellious children and responds to their cries.

PRAYER: Lord, I will turn to you whenever I face a crisis. Thank you for your faithful support. Amen.

Jehoash, son of Jehoahaz, King of Israel

Soldiers in modern armies are paid a salary by the government, but they also often oppress their victims. In ancient times, a soldier's pay was often plunder of the defeated. Jehoash thought his enemy's treasure was his rightful reward for winning a war.

Jehoash reigned in Israel from about 798 to 782 BC.[8] He was an evil king like his father and grandfather.

Amaziah, King of Judah, thought his army was strong, so he challenged Jehoash to a battle. Jehoash tried to discourage him from breaking the peace.

> [After threatening back and forth,] Amaziah [King of Judah] would not listen, so King Jehoash of Israel advanced. He and King Amaziah of Judah met face to face at Beth-shemesh that belonged to Judah. Judah was routed before Israel, and each man fled to his own tent. King Jehoash of Israel captured Judah's King Amaziah son of Joash, son of Ahaziah, at Beth-shemesh. Then Jehoash went to Jerusalem and broke down two hundred yards of Jerusalem's wall from the Ephraim Gate to the Corner Gate. He took all the gold and silver, all the articles found in the Lord's temple and in the treasuries of the king's palace, and some hostages. Then he returned to Samaria.
>
> 2 Kings 14:11–14 (CSB)

---

[8]Jehoash was also called Joash. 2 Kings 13:10–25; 14:7-16.

King Jehoash defeated the army of Judah and captured King Amaziah. Then Jehoash demolished some of Jerusalem's wall and plundered the Lord's temple and the king's palace.

Sometimes church leaders misuse church funds for selfish purposes. This amounts to plundering God's people, like Jehoash plundered the Lord's temple.

> But sexual immorality and any impurity or greed should not even be heard of among you, as is proper for saints.
>
> Ephesians 5:3 (CSB)

Greed is normal in modern society, but greed is sin which leads to all kinds of evil actions.

> PRAYER: Lord, test my heart, so I don't fall into a greedy attitude. Amen.

Amaziah, son of Joash, King of Judah

When someone is murdered, it is important for justice to be done. A stable society depends upon fair and effective police and courts. Amaziah was careful to administer justice as prescribed by the Law.

Amaziah reigned in Judah from about 796 to 767 BC.[9] He followed the Lord as his father had. However, the people continued to worship idols on high places. When he learned of a conspiracy in Jerusalem, he fled to Lachish, but he was assassinated there.

> As soon as the kingdom was firmly in his grasp, Amaziah killed his servants who had killed his father the king [Joash]. However, he did not put the children of the killers to death, as it is written in the book of the law of Moses where the Lord commanded, "Fathers are not to be put to death because of children,

---

[9] 2 Kings 14:1–20.

and children are not to be put to death because of fathers; instead, each one will be put to death for his own sin."

2 Kings 14:5–6 (CSB)

Those who assassinated King Amaziah's father, King Joash, received the death penalty. Most ancient kings would have also killed the families of rebels, but King Amaziah followed the law of Moses. Justice means only the ones who sin are punished.

At the last judgment, God will judge each person for his own sin. The sin of relatives will not be an excuse. The fact Mom and Dad went to church won't matter. Each person is responsible for his own actions, words, and thoughts.

I also saw the dead, the great and the small, standing before the throne, and books were opened. Another book was opened, which is the book of life, and the dead were judged according to their works by what was written in the books.

Revelation 20:12 (CSB)

Those who have faith in Jesus will find their penalty has already been paid by Jesus. Their sins are forgiven.

PRAYER: Lord, thank you for forgiving me of my sins. Amen.

Jeroboam, son of Jehoash, King of Israel

When I'm faced with a crisis, I don't care who the Lord uses to answer my prayers. They don't have be righteous. Jeroboam was a successful military leader, even though he continued idol worship in Israel.

Jeroboam reigned in Israel from about 793 to 753 BC.[10] He was coregent with his father for some years.

---

[10] 2 Kings 14:23–29.

62

> [King Jeroboam] restored Israel's border from Lebo-hamath as far as the Sea of the Arabah, according to the word the Lord, the God of Israel, had spoken through his servant, the prophet Jonah son of Amittai from Gath-hepher. For the Lord saw that the affliction of Israel was very bitter for both slaves and free people. There was no one to help Israel. The Lord had not said he would blot out the name of Israel under heaven, so he delivered them by the hand of Jeroboam son of Jehoash.
>
> 2 Kings 14:25–27 (CSB)

King Jeroboam restored Israel's borders to a similar extent as Solomon's kingdom to the north and east. Jeroboam was a deliverer from oppression, even though he continued the worship of gold calves and other idols begun by King Jeroboam, son of Nebat. Jonah, son of Amittai, was the Lord's prophet to Israel at this time.[11]

God's purpose for his people does not depend on whether he uses a good or evil person. Sometimes worldly people are instrumental in answering my prayers.

For example, evil men were the instrument for Paul's trip to Rome. Going to Rome was God's plan, even though Paul went as a prisoner.

> When it was decided that we were to sail to Italy, they handed over Paul and some other prisoners to a centurion named Julius, of the Imperial Regiment.
>
> Acts 27:1 (CSB)

Another example: when I was about to be drafted into the army, I prayed I would not go to Vietnam. Due to politics, worldly people in Congress delayed the draft and my draft board allowed further delays until the war was almost over, so even though I was forced into the army, I did not go to Vietnam.

> PRAYER: Lord, thank you for guiding my life and answering my prayers. Amen.

---

[11] The book of Jonah is about his mission to Nineveh.

Azariah, son of Amaziah, King of Judah

Pride comes easy for me. Maybe I think I'm smarter than the next guy. But the slogan, "Pride goes before a fall"[12] is true. I've experienced it over and over. Azariah made an arrogant mistake too.

Azariah (also called Uzziah) reigned in Judah from about 791 to 739 BC.[13] He was coregent with his father for some years.

> The Lord afflicted the king, [Azariah,] and he had a serious skin disease until the day of his death. He lived in quarantine, while Jotham, the king's son, was over the household—governing the people of the land.
>
> 2 Kings 15:5 (CSB)

King Azariah was afflicted with a skin disease,[14] because he tried to burn incense to the Lord in the temple. Only priests were allowed to do this. Quarantine was required for skin diseases, so his son had to do the public governing duties for his father.

Azariah was commended in general for doing what was right, but this incident had bad consequences for him.

> All of you clothe yourselves with humility toward one another, because
> God resists the proud
> but gives grace to the humble.
> Humble yourselves, therefore, under the mighty hand of God, so that he may exalt you at the proper time.
>
> 1 Peter 5:5–6 (CSB)

Similar to Azariah, my arrogance leads to embarrassment when I'm proven wrong. I must ask the Lord for forgiveness. Life goes better when I embrace humility.

PRAYER: Lord, help me to embrace humility in all my relationships. Amen.

---

[12]Proverbs 16:18.

[13]2 Kings 15:1–7 and 2 Chronicles 26:16–21.

[14]The Hebrew word translated "leprosy" also includes other skin diseases besides Hansen's disease.

Zechariah, son of Jeroboam, King of Israel

Governments today seem to be lacking truth, righteousness, and justice. A dynasty will not endure if they continue to ignore what the Lord requires. Zechariah was the last of Jehu's dynasty.

Zechariah reigned in Israel for six months in 753 BC.[15] He was assassinated.

> Nevertheless, the Lord said to Jehu, "Because you have done well in carrying out what is right in my sight and have done to the house of Ahab all that was in my heart, four generations of your sons will sit on the throne of Israel."
>
> 2 Kings 10:30 (CSB)

> The word of the Lord that he spoke to Jehu was, "Four generations of your sons will sit on the throne of Israel," and it was so.
>
> 2 Kings 15:12 (CSB)

King Zechariah was the fourth generation of King Jehu's descendants. Jehu was commended by God for destroying Omri's dynasty, including Ahab's descendants. Jehu succeeded in eliminating Baal worship from Israel, but he did not get rid of the gold calves and other idols that Jeroboam, son of Nebat, had set up. He followed the Lord only half way. Thus, God limited Jehu's dynasty. Zechariah was an evil king like all those before him. He reigned six months and was assassinated.

Following the Lord half way never produces lasting results. King David is my example. He followed the Lord whole heartedly.

> You reveal the path of life to me;
> in your presence is abundant joy;
> at your right hand are eternal pleasures.
>
> Psalm 16:11 (CSB)

> PRAYER: Lord, like David, show me your path, so I can live that way. Amen.

---

[15] 2 Kings 15:8–12.

6

The era of the final kings of Israel (752–722 BC)

The Neo-Assyrian Empire lasted from 911 to 609 BC. The Assyrian king, Tiglath-Pileser III, began a period of aggressive military conquest in 745 BC which affected the era of the final kings of Israel. At its height, the Assyrian Empire was the strongest military power in the world. Many consider it to be the first world empire.

This chapter includes devotional meditations on the following: the kings of Israel who reigned during this time; and the kings of Judah who began their reigns during this time. This era ended when Samaria, the capital of Israel, was conquered by Assyria. The king was imprisoned and the people of Israel were deported. This ended Israel as a nation.

Shallum, son of Jabesh, King of Israel

Some video games depict the action of warfare, the excitement of explosions, and the stealth of assassinating enemies. Everyone knows video games are pretend. Shallum was a real assassin.

Shallum reigned in Israel for only one month in 752 BC.[1] He was assassinated.

---

[1] 2 Kings 15:10,13–15.

> Shallum son of Jabesh conspired against Zechariah. He struck him down publicly, killed him, and became king in his place.
>
> 2 Kings 15:10 (CSB)

Shallum continued the practice of conspiring and assassinating kings. He did this in plain sight of the people and seized the throne.

Instead of assassination, Jesus had a different way to deal with enemies.

> You have heard that it was said, Love your neighbor and hate your enemy. But I tell you, love your enemies and pray for those who persecute you.
>
> Matthew 5:43–44 (CSB)

Too often I hear of churchgoers who conspire against the pastor. Their hatred is like an assassination.[2] Loving each other is more important than controversies. Jesus told us to love even our enemies.

> PRAYER: Lord, help me be a peacemaker when there is a controversy at church. Amen.

Jotham, son of Azariah, King of Judah

There is a place in the back of one's eye that does not process light. It causes a blind spot in that eye's vision. Jotham had a spiritual blind spot.

Jotham reigned in Judah from about 752 to 736 BC.[3] He was coregent with his father for some years.

> [King Jotham] did what was right in the Lord's sight just as his father Uzziah [Azariah] had done. Yet the high places were not taken away; the people continued sacrificing and burning incense on the high places.
>
> 2 Kings 15:34–35 (CSB)

---

[2] 1 John 3:15.
[3] 2 Kings 15:32–38.

King Solomon and his son King Rehoboam set up altars and idols on high places to worship like the Canaanites had. A few kings of Judah had removed the altars, but they were promptly rebuilt. Most of Judah's kings over the next centuries let the people keep worshiping on high places. King Jotham was no different, even though, in general, Jotham was a good king. He was careful to obey the Law and worship the Lord in Jerusalem.

The Pharasees in Jesus time were careful to do what the Law specified, but ignored more important issues. They had blind spots.

> Woe to you, scribes and Pharisees, hypocrites! You pay a tenth of mint, dill, and cumin, and yet you have neglected the more important matters of the law— justice, mercy, and faithfulness.
>
> Matthew 23:23 (CSB)

Modern Christians are often similar to Jotham who tolerated traditional idolatry. For example, a church may be very careful how they conduct worship services, yet ignore greedy attitudes by the members. Most Christians want to do what the Bible teaches, but often have blind spots, excusing some sinful practices and attitudes.

PRAYER: Lord, show me my spiritual blind spots. Amen.

Menahem, son of Gadi, King of Israel

When faced with an overwhelming threat, a person has to find a way to survive. Should I fight or flee? Menahem faced an overwhelming Assyrian invasion.

Menahem reigned in Israel from about 751 to 742 BC.[4] He became king after assassinating King Shallum.

---

[4] 2 Kings 15:14–22.

> King Pul [Tiglath-Pileser] of Assyria invaded the land, so Menahem gave Pul seventy-five thousand pounds [1,000 talents] of silver so that Pul would support him to strengthen his grasp on the kingdom. Then Menahem exacted twenty ounces [50 shekels] of silver from each of the prominent men of Israel to give to the king of Assyria. So the king of Assyria withdrew and did not stay there in the land.
>
> 2 Kings 15:19–20 (CSB)

King Menahem heavily taxed Israel's prominent citizens to bribe the invading Assyrian army so they would leave Israel's territory. He relied on bribery to maintain his reign.

The world thinks that bribes will ensure loyalty. This often works for a while because most people are selfish and greedy. However, the Kingdom of God is upheld by servant leaders and love for people, instead of bribery.

> [To elders:] Shepherd God's flock among you, not overseeing out of compulsion but willingly, as God would have you; not out of greed for money but eagerly; not lording it over those entrusted to you, but being examples to the flock.
>
> 1 Peter 5:2–3 (CSB)

My goal is to live as a citizen of God's Kingdom. If I am leading younger believers, then I must have pure motives and actions.

> PRAYER: Lord, help me to keep my motives and actions pure. Amen.

Pekahiah, son of Menahem, King of Israel

Everyone has personal traditions. For example, "I cook my ham this way, because that's how my mother did it." Some traditions are helpful, some are innocent, and some are destructive. Pekahiah continued traditional idolatry in Israel.

Pekahiah reigned in Israel from about 741 to 740 BC.[5] He reigned about two years and then was assassinated.

> [King Pekahiah] reigned two years. He did what was evil in the Lord's sight and did not turn away from the sins Jeroboam son of Nebat had caused Israel to commit.
>
> 2 Kings 15:23–24 (CSB)

King Jeroboam, son of Nebat, set up gold calf idols for the people to worship instead of letting them worship the Lord in Jerusalem. He also set up altars and idols on high places for worship similar to those used by the Canaanites. Over the next two hundred years, every king of Israel continued the idolatry begun by Jeroboam. Pekahiah was no different.

Once a false doctrine becomes entrenched in a church denomination or movement, it is very difficult to uproot. Jesus reproved the church in Pergamum for false doctrine.

> But I have a few things against you. You have some there who hold to the teaching of Balaam, who taught Balak to place a stumbling block in front of the Israelites: to eat meat sacrificed to idols and to commit sexual immorality. In the same way, you also have those who hold to the teaching of the Nicolaitans. So repent! Otherwise, I will come to you quickly and fight against them with the sword of my mouth.
>
> Revelation 2:14–16 (CSB)

Even though the people in Pergamum were faithful, Jesus demanded they repent from the immorality that flowed from the false doctrine.

> PRAYER: Lord, show me where I cling to false doctrine. Amen.

---

[5] 2 Kings 15:23–26.

Pekah, son of Remaliah, King of Israel

Sometimes the activities of life get disorganized and my plans fall apart. I may face circumstances I have no control over. I may lose my job, or friends may move away. Pekah's plans fell apart as his kingdom began to disintegrate.

Pekah reigned in Israel from about 740 to 732 BC.[6] He was assassinated.

> In the days of King Pekah of Israel, King Tiglath-Pileser of Assyria came and captured Ijon, Abel-beth-maacah, Janoah, Kedesh, Hazor, Gilead, and Galilee—all the land of Naphtali—and deported the people to Assyria.
>
> 2 Kings 15:29 (CSB)

During King Pekah's reign, Assyria began to capture territory of Israel and deport the people. The Lord was getting fed up with their idolatry. Pekah's reign began the dissolution of Israel as a nation.

Local churches can face dissolution, like Israel did. Jesus warned five of seven churches in the Roman province of Asia to repent.[7] If they did not, they would be removed from God's presence. Modern churches face the same issues as Israel and the churches described in Revelation.

> Remember then how far you have fallen; repent, and do the works you did at first. Otherwise, I will come to you and remove your lampstand from its place, unless you repent.
>
> Revelation 2:5 (CSB)

Idolatry by God's people eventually brings judgment. Modern idols may not be statues made of wood or stone, but things that demand my loyalty are like idols. For example, early in my career, my employer demanded that I work long overtime hours.

---

[6] 2 Kings 15:25–31. Dating kings is difficult.
[7] Revelation 1:10–3:22.

They were expecting me to worship the company. Being a reliable employee didn't mean worshiping the company. I had to put the Lord first.

> PRAYER: Lord, help me see clearly how to put you first in every situation. Amen.

Ahaz, son of Jotham, King of Judah

Some people try to follow the latest fashion trends. They dress like a photo in a magazine or a video on-line. Their speech is sprinkled with the latest slogans. They advocate the ideas of the rich and famous. Ahaz adopted the latest religious ideas.

Ahaz reigned in Judah from about 736 to 720 BC.[8] Assyria conquered Israel in 722 BC during Ahaz's reign.

> [King Ahaz] walked in the ways of the kings of Israel. He even sacrificed his son in the fire, imitating the detestable practices of the nations the Lord had dispossessed before the Israelites. He sacrificed and burned incense on the high places, on the hills, and under every green tree...
>
> King Ahaz went to Damascus to meet King Tiglath-Pileser of Assyria. When he saw the altar that was in Damascus, King Ahaz sent a model of the altar and complete plans for its construction to the priest Uriah.
>
> Uriah built the altar according to all the instructions King Ahaz sent from Damascus. Therefore, by the time King Ahaz came back from Damascus, the priest Uriah had completed it.
>
> When the king came back from Damascus, he saw the altar. Then he approached the altar and ascended it. He offered his burnt offering and his grain offering, poured out his drink offering, and splattered the blood of his fellowship offerings on the altar.
>
> 2 Kings 16:3–13 (CSB)

---

[8] 2 Kings 16:1–20.

Unlike his father, King Ahaz worshiped like the Canaanites at the high places and by sacrificing his children. Moreover, when he went to Damascus to meet the king of Assyria, he saw an impressive altar and sent plans for the altar back home. When the king came back from Damascus, he presented offerings on the new altar himself in the temple courtyard. Only priests were supposed to offer sacrifices to the Lord. Ahaz wanted to be like the powerful pagan kings who acted as both priests and rulers.

King Ahaz was a very religious person. He probably thought the ancient Canaanites knew how to please the local gods. He also worshiped the Lord with the very latest pagan religious equipment. He thought an exotic altar made him look good. However, it was not what the Lord demanded.

The people of Athens enjoyed debating exotic religious ideas. When Paul visited Athens he debated with some of the philosophers there. Jesus' resurrection sounded strange to them.

> [Paul] was telling the good news about Jesus and the resurrection... Now all the Athenians and the foreigners residing there spent their time on nothing else but telling or hearing something new...
>
> Acts 17:16–34 (CSB)

Like Ahaz, some modern churchgoers adopt religious ideas and practices from Hindu, Buddhist, and Native American cultures. Exotic ideas and religious practices are essentially pagan worship, even though they may be done in a church building. They forget that Jesus is the center of Christianity. Obedience to him is more important than the latest religious fad.

PRAYER: Lord, help me to see religious fads with your eyes and to concentrate on what is important. Amen.

Hoshea, son of Elah, King of Israel

People today often forget that a loan or a credit card purchase is a promise to repay promptly. They think it is okay to skip a payment when it is inconvenient. Hoshea skipped payments to Assyria.

Hoshea reigned in Israel from about 732 to 722 BC.[9] He was seized by Shalmaneser, King of Assyria, and imprisoned. The fall of his capital Samaria marked the end of Israel's existence as a nation.

> The king of Assyria caught Hoshea in a conspiracy: He had sent envoys to So king of Egypt and had not paid tribute to the king of Assyria as in previous years. Therefore the king of Assyria arrested him and put him in prison. The king of Assyria invaded the whole land, marched up to Samaria, and besieged it for three years.
>
> 2 Kings 17:4–5 (CSB)

Hoshea became king after he assassinated King Pekah. He was supposed to be a vassal of Assyria, but he discontinued payments to Assyria and tried to get Egypt to help him. His plot failed; he was imprisoned; and his nation was conquered and deported.

> Pay your obligations to everyone: taxes to those you owe taxes, tolls to those you owe tolls, respect to those you owe respect, and honor to those you owe honor.
>
> Romans 13:7 (CSB)

When I make promises to a superior, failure to fulfill them can have drastic consequences. For example, if I don't pay the electric company, they will cut off my electricity. If I don't pay my rent, I will be evicted and end up on the street. Telling the truth is important to the Lord. Thus, he expects me to do what I promised.

> PRAYER: Lord, help me to always do what I promised, especially in my finances. Amen.

---

[9] 2 Kings 15:30; 17:1–6.

7

The era of the final kings of Judah (729–586 BC)

The Neo-Babylonian Empire was firmly established when the Medes and Babylonians conquered the Assyrian capital Nineveh in 612 BC, effectively taking over the Assyrian empire. Babylon defeated Egypt at the battle of Carchemish in 605 BC. This resulted in Babylon dominating the land of Judah instead of Egypt.

This chapter includes devotional meditations on the following: the kings of Judah who reigned during this time, beginning with Hezekiah; and a few other people. This era ended when Jerusalem, the capital of Judah, was conquered by Babylon. The king was imprisoned and the people of Judah were deported. This ended Judah as a nation.

Hezekiah, son of Ahaz, King of Judah

A young adult has to decide whether to follow in his father's footsteps. Most fathers are good examples in some respects and not in others. Hezekiah rejected the idols and traditions of his father and was faithful to the Lord like his ancestor David.

Hezekiah reigned in Judah from about 729 to 699 BC.[1] He was coregent with his father for some years.

---

[1] 2 Kings 18:1–20:21.

[King Hezekiah] did what was right in the Lord's sight just as his ancestor David had done. He removed the high places, shattered the sacred pillars, and cut down the Asherah poles. He broke into pieces the bronze snake that Moses made, for until then the Israelites were burning incense to it. It was called Nehushtan. Hezekiah relied on the Lord God of Israel; not one of the kings of Judah was like him, either before him or after him. He remained faithful to the Lord and did not turn from following him but kept the commands the Lord had commanded Moses. The Lord was with him, and wherever he went he prospered.

2 Kings 18:3–7 (CSB)

King Hezekiah removed the idols and pagan practices of his father Ahaz. He even removed the shrines at high places which many of Judah's kings had tolerated. He was commended for his faithfulness in the face of aggression by Assyria.

Do not love the world or the things in the world. If anyone loves the world, the love of the Father is not in him. For everything in the world—the lust of the flesh, the lust of the eyes, and the pride in one's possessions—is not from the Father, but is from the world. And the world with its lust is passing away, but the one who does the will of God remains forever.

1 John 2:15–17 (CSB)

Hezekiah's life is a good example for today's believer, beginning with repudiation of idols in modern society. Some idols, like the high places, are embedded in traditions. Some, like the Asherah poles, are about immoral sexuality. Some, like the bronze snake, were part of a good story in the past, but have become idols. Like Hezekiah, I will turn away from idols in modern society.

PRAYER: Lord, help me recognize the idols of modern society. Amen.

Hezekiah healed

I'm told that a responsible person in modern society should prepare for death by writing a will. That way his family will know what they are supposed to do with his possessions. Hezekiah was told to make such preparations.

> In those days Hezekiah became terminally ill. The prophet Isaiah son of Amoz came and said to him, "This is what the Lord says: 'Set your house in order, for you are about to die; you will not recover.' "
>
> Then Hezekiah turned his face to the wall and prayed to the Lord, "Please, Lord, remember how I have walked before you faithfully and wholeheartedly and have done what pleases you." And Hezekiah wept bitterly.
>
> Isaiah had not yet gone out of the inner courtyard when the word of the Lord came to him: "Go back and tell Hezekiah, the leader of my people, 'This is what the Lord God of your ancestor David says: I have heard your prayer; I have seen your tears. Look, I will heal you.' "
>
> 2 Kings 20:1–5 (CSB)

When Hezekiah became very ill, the prophet Isaiah[2] told him he was about to die, so he should put his affairs in order.[3] Naturally, Hezekiah did not want to die, so he prayed earnestly. The Lord told Isaiah he would answer Hezekiah's prayer. The Lord also revealed to Isaiah what to do to Hezekiah's wound. He was healed and he lived another fifteen years.

Hezekiah's example illustrates the importance of prayer. The Lord's response illustrates his love for his children, his power over sickness, and his wisdom in practical helps. The New Testament also tells us to pray for the sick.

---

[2]Isaiah, son of Amoz, wrote the book of Isaiah.
[3]2 Kings 20:1–11.

> Is anyone among you sick? He should call for the
> elders of the church, and they are to pray over him,
> anointing him with oil in the name of the Lord. The
> prayer of faith will save the sick person, and the Lord
> will raise him up.
>
> James 5:14–18 (CSB)

Gifts of the Holy Spirit include healings, words of wisdom, and words of knowledge, which I think includes medical wisdom and medical knowledge.[4] All of these glorify God and help believers.

> PRAYER: Lord, thank you for the medical knowledge
> and wisdom you have blessed the world with, but
> most of all, thank you for the healing gifts of the Holy
> Spirit that apply to me. Amen.

Sennacherib, King of Assyria

Many people today think they don't need religion. They rely on themselves. They don't realize the creator of the universe is who they need. Sennacherib thought he was more powerful than any local god.

Sennacherib ruled Assyria from about 705 to 681 BC. He invaded Judah in about 701 BC, because King Hezekiah had rebelled and had not paid tribute.[5] Even though Hezekiah tried to pay him to leave Judah, Sennacherib was determined to deport the rebellious Judeans. While he was fighting other cities, he sent two high officials, his spokesman, and an army to Jerusalem. His spokesman delivered an ultimatum to the people in Jerusalem.

> [The spokesman for the king of Assyria shouted,]
> "Don't listen to Hezekiah when he misleads you, saying, 'The Lord will rescue us.' Has any of the gods
> of the nations ever rescued his land from the power

---

[4] 1 Corinthians 12:8–9.
[5] 2 Kings 18:13–19:37.

of the king of Assyria? Where are the gods of Hamath and Arpad? Where are the gods of Sepharvaim, Hena, and Ivvah? Have they rescued Samaria from my power? Who among all the gods of the lands has rescued his land from my power? So will the Lord rescue Jerusalem from my power?"

2 Kings 18:32–35 (CSB)

When Hezekiah's officials reported what the Assyrian spokesman had said, Hezekiah tore his clothes in mourning, went into the temple to pray, and sent his officials to the prophet Isaiah.[6]

Isaiah told them not to be afraid of the Assyrians who had blasphemed the Lord. Sennacherib repeated his ultimatum in a written message to Hezekiah.

Hezekiah took the letter from the [Assyrian] messengers' hands, read it, then went up to the Lord's temple, and spread it out before the Lord. Then Hezekiah prayed before the Lord...

2 Kings 19:14–15 (CSB)

Hezekiah prayed, pointing out that the gods of the other nations were just impotent idols. He concluded his prayer saying, "Now, Lord our God, please save us from his power so that all the kingdoms of the earth may know that you, Lord, are God—you alone."

Isaiah sent Hezekiah the Lord's reply. He concluded, "I will defend this city and rescue it for my sake and for the sake of my servant David."

That night, the Lord struck the camp of the Assyrians. There were dead bodies everywhere. So, Sennacherib and his army returned to his home in Nineveh.

Sennacherib thought the God of Judah was just a local god. He arrogantly assumed he was stronger than any local god. He did not realize he was blaspheming the creator of the universe, the only true God.

---

[6]The book of Isaiah has a parallel passage. Isaiah 36:1–37:38.

People today, like Sennacherib, often think they can solve all of life's challenges by their own efforts. They may brag about past accomplishments. They may think an army of supporters will overcome all opposition. They may blaspheme in their rage. They may issue ultimatums. But believers know the creator of the universe.

> Submit to God. Resist the devil, and he will flee from you. Draw near to God, and he will draw near to you... Humble yourselves before the Lord, and he will exalt you.
>
> James 4:7–10 (CSB)

Like Hezekiah, believers humbly pray to the Lord for deliverance. They know a relationship with the Lord is the solution to all of life's challenges.

> PRAYER: Lord, thank you for deliverance from enemies. Amen.

Workmen in the tunnel

King Hezekiah's workmen carved a tunnel through solid rock from the Gihon Spring to the Pool of Siloam.[7] The spring is on the cliff above the Kidron Valley. The pool of Siloam was within the walls of Jerusalem. The tunnel and defenses prevented an invader from accessing the spring water. The curving tunnel is 583 yards long. The tunnel was explored by archaeologists in the 1800s and is a tourist site today.

> The rest of the events of Hezekiah's reign, along with all his might and how he made the pool and the tunnel and brought water into the city, are written in the Historical Record of Judah's Kings. Hezekiah rested with his ancestors, and his son Manasseh became king in his place.
>
> 2 Kings 20:20–21 (CSB)

---

[7] 2 Chronicles 32:2–4,30.

I wonder what the workmen thought who chipped through solid rock to make Hezekiah's tunnel. "This is too hard!" "This is crazy!" It must have been difficult to know which direction to go. Tradition says two teams worked from each end. Mistakes were made and the tunnel turns this way and that. Eventually, the teams met underground.

Following the guidance of the Holy Spirit often seems too hard. Progress is slow, just chipping away at obstacles. Which direction should I go?

> I say, then, walk by the Spirit and you will certainly not carry out the desire of the flesh...But if you are led by the Spirit, you are not under the law.
>
> Galatians 5:16–18 (CSB)

Eventually, I will arrive at his destination for me and my path may help someone else draw living water from the Lord.

> PRAYER: Lord, thank you for leading me by your Holy Spirit. Amen.

Manasseh, son of Hezekiah, King of Judah

Even though a reformer like King Hezekiah may reign for a long time, corruption can easily gain a foothold. Manasseh reintroduced pagan practices in Judah.

Manasseh reigned in Judah from about 698 to 643 BC, beginning when he was twelve years old.[8]

> [King Manasseh] did what was evil in the Lord's sight, imitating the detestable practices of the nations that the Lord had dispossessed before the Israelites. He rebuilt the high places that his father Hezekiah had destroyed and reestablished the altars for Baal. He made an Asherah, as King Ahab of Israel had done; he also bowed in worship to all the stars in the sky

[8] 2 Kings 21:1–18.

and served them. He built altars in the Lord's temple, where the Lord had said, "Jerusalem is where I will put my name." He built altars to all the stars in the sky in both courtyards of the Lord's temple. He sacrificed his son in the fire, practiced witchcraft and divination, and consulted mediums and spiritists. He did a huge amount of evil in the Lord's sight, angering him.

Manasseh set up the carved image of Asherah, which he made, in the temple... Manasseh caused [Judah] to stray so that they did worse evil than the nations the Lord had destroyed before the Israelites.

2 Kings 21:2–9 (CSB)

King Manasseh reversed the reforms done by his father Hezekiah and worse. He rebuilt the high places and worshiped Baal, Asherah, and the stars. He profaned the temple of the Lord by putting altars and idols there. He sacrificed his son and practiced witchcraft, divination, and necromancy. The idolatry of Judah was worse than the ancient Canaanites. The Lord's prophets proclaimed how the Lord was determined to judge Judah.

Manasseh is an example of a corrupt leader using his long tenure to corrupt his people. Often moral compromises are made gradually, becoming worse than the pagans. God's judgment of Judah is a warning to church organizations today.

There were indeed false prophets among the people [of ancient Israel], just as there will be false teachers among you. They will bring in destructive heresies, even denying the Master who bought them, and will bring swift destruction on themselves. Many will follow their depraved ways, and the way of truth will be maligned because of them.

2 Peter 2:1–2 (CSB)

No matter what leaders may do or say, I will remain loyal to the Lord and to what his Word, the Bible, teaches.

PRAYER: Lord, give me discernment to recognize false teachers and corrupt leaders. Amen.

Amon, son of Manasseh, King of Judah

When a young person leaves home, he tends to worship in the same type of church as his parents. It is familiar. The songs are the same. The order of service is the same. It is comfortable. Amon continued to worship like his father had.

Amon reigned in Judah from about 642 to 640 BC.[9] He was assassinated by his servants in his own house.

> [King Amon] did what was evil in the Lord's sight, just as his father Manasseh had done. He walked in all the ways his father had walked; he served the idols his father had served, and he bowed in worship to them. He abandoned the Lord God of his ancestors and did not walk in the ways of the Lord.
>
> 2 Kings 21:20–22 (CSB)

Amon reigned only two years. During that short time, he worshiped all the idols his father Manasseh had established. He did not return to the Lord.

A young man chooses who he will imitate. Will he look to a godly relative or friend, or to a worldly one? For example, Paul became a mentor to Timothy.

> Paul went on to Derbe and Lystra, where there was a disciple named Timothy, the son of a believing Jewish woman, but his father was a Greek. The brothers and sisters at Lystra and Iconium spoke highly of him. Paul wanted Timothy to go with him; so he took him and circumcised him because of the Jews who were in those places, since they all knew that his father was a Greek.
>
> Acts 16:1–3 (CSB)

When I was in my twenties, like Amon, there were godly men I met at my local church who were mentors for me.

> PRAYER: Lord, thank you for the godly role models you gave me. Amen.

[9]2 Kings 21:19–26.

85

Josiah, son of Amon, King of Judah

I began reading the Bible for myself when I was about twelve years old. I wanted to find out what God said. Josiah didn't know what the Bible said until he was about twenty-six years old. He was shocked.

Josiah reigned in Judah from about 640 to 609 BC.[10] He was only eight years old when he was crowned king. He did what was right, like his ancestor David. His steadfast devotion to the Lord was more than any of the kings of Judah. He was wounded in battle against Egypt and died.

When he was about twenty-six years old, he ordered that workmen clean and repair the Lord's temple. While the work was going on, Hilkiah, the high priest, reported to Josiah's officials, "I have found the book of the Law in the Lord's temple."

> Then the court secretary Shaphan told the king [Josiah], "The priest Hilkiah has given me a book," and Shaphan read it in the presence of the king. When the king heard the words of the book of the law, he tore his clothes.
>
> 2 Kings 22:10–11 (CSB)

> In addition, Josiah eradicated the mediums, the spiritists, household idols, images, and all the abhorrent things that were seen in the land of Judah and in Jerusalem. He did this in order to carry out the words of the law that were written in the book that the priest Hilkiah found in the Lord's temple.
>
> 2 Kings 23:24 (CSB)

Apparently, the book of the Law had been ignored ever since Hezekiah's reign. When it was read to him, King Josiah heard the curses against idolatry and the other sins Judah had been doing, so he tore his clothes in repentance. He mandated a thorough cleansing of the priests and Levites, the temple, the cities, and the land, including the area of former Israel. He even removed the

---

[10]2 Kings 21:24–23:30.

gold calf and its altar in Bethel which Jeroboam, son of Nebat, had set up.

Like Josiah, I am thankful for the Bible, the Word of God. The Bible clearly distinguishes sin and righteousness. Reading it makes the consequences of sin plain. Through Jesus, God's solution to sin is repentance. He forgives sin.

> All Scripture is inspired by God and is profitable for teaching, for rebuking, for correcting, for training in righteousness, so that the man of God may be complete, equipped for every good work.
> 2 Timothy 3:16–17 (CSB)

Josiah's attitude is a good example for Christians today. He repented for his nation; so will I. He removed idols; so will I. He loved the Lord with all of his heart, soul, and strength; so will I.

> PRAYER: Lord, thank you for the example of Josiah, especially how he loved you. Amen.

Passover participant

The Passover festival was prescribed by Moses, so the Israelites would remember what God did for them. The first Passover set them free from Egyptian slavery.[11]

> The king [Josiah] commanded all the people, "Observe the Passover of the Lord your God as written in the book of the covenant." No such Passover had ever been observed from the time of the judges who judged Israel through the entire time of the kings of Israel and Judah. But in the eighteenth year of King Josiah, the Lord's Passover was observed in Jerusalem.
> 2 Kings 23:21–23 (CSB)

---

[11]Exodus 12:1–31 and Deuteronomy 16:1–8.

After cleansing the land of idols and renewing the covenant between the people and the Lord, Josiah ordered that everyone observe the Passover festival. Each family had roasted lamb or goat for dinner with unleavened bread. I wonder what an average guy thought about the Passover and all Josiah's reforms. It must have seemed strange. Perhaps he realized, "Oh, we really are the Lord's people!"

My church hosted a sedar dinner which combined traditional Jewish customs with some New Testament interpretation. The ceremony was very moving. The exodus story hits one's heart. Realizing Jesus is the Lamb of God in a fresh way makes me extra thankful.

> The next day John [the Baptist] saw Jesus coming toward him and said, "Look, the Lamb of God, who takes away the sin of the world!"
>
> John 1:29 (CSB)

> PRAYER: Lord, thank you for sending Jesus to be the Lamb of God who took away my sins. Amen.

Jehoahaz, son of Josiah, King of Judah

Many college students abandon the religion of their parents after they arrive on campus. Saturday night parties become more important than church on Sunday. Jehoahaz abandoned the faith of his father Josiah.

Jehoahaz reigned in Judah in 609 BC.[12] He reigned for only three months. He was deposed by Pharaoh Neco who took him to Egypt where he died. Judah was losing its independence.

> [King Jehoahaz] did what was evil in the Lord's sight just as his ancestors had done.
>
> 2 Kings 23:32 (CSB)

---

[12] 2 Kings 23:31–34.

King Jehoahaz reverted to the idolatry of his grandfather Amon and great grandfather Manasseh during his short reign. He was twenty-three years old. Apparently the reforms of Josiah were not taken to heart by most of the people.

When a church has a spiritual awakening, like the reforms of Josiah, there is fresh devotion and enthusiasm. However, after a while, people feel exhausted. Worship services become spiritually stale. It is easy to fall back into old patterns. For example, Jesus rebuked the church in Sardis for their old dead patterns.

> I know your works; you have a reputation for being alive, but you are dead. Be alert and strengthen what remains, which is about to die, for I have not found your works complete before my God.
>
> Revelation 3:1–2 (CSB)

Even if others become stale, I must keep my personal devotion strong. I am praying for lasting change in my community.

> PRAYER: Lord, send revival to my city, my county, that will permanently change us. Amen.

Jehoiakim, son of Josiah, King of Judah

Investors are always interested in economic forecasts. "Will interest rates go up? Will there be a recession?" The Lord's prophets, like Jeremiah,[13] kept warning Jehoiakim of the coming disaster.

Jehoiakim reigned in Judah from about 609 to 598 BC.[14] Pharaoh Neco appointed Jehoiakim to be king in place of his brother Jehoahaz. He died shortly before King Nebuchadnezzar of Babylon exiled the royal family and officials to Babylon.

> [King Jehoiakim] did what was evil in the Lord's sight just as his ancestors had done.
>
> During Jehoiakim's reign, King Nebuchadnezzar of Babylon attacked. Jehoiakim became his vassal for

---

[13]Jeremiah 1:1–3.
[14]2 Kings 23:34–24:7.

three years, and then he turned and rebelled against him. The Lord sent Chaldean, Aramean, Moabite, and Ammonite raiders against Jehoiakim. He sent them against Judah to destroy it, according to the word of the Lord he had spoken through his servants the prophets.

2 Kings 23:37; 24:1–2 (CSB)

King Jehoiakim continued the idolatry established by Manasseh. Even though Josiah had made reforms, the Lord's judgment against Judah was still pending. Judgment began under Jehoiakim. Judah had lost its independence as a nation and raiders savaged the people.

Rebelling against the Lord never turns out well. Sin brings death in many ways. This applies to nations, churches, families, and individuals.

For the wages of sin is death, but the gift of God is eternal life in Christ Jesus our Lord.

Romans 6:23 (CSB)

PRAYER: Lord, thank you for the gift of eternal life because of Jesus. Amen.

Jehoiachin, son of Jehoiakim, King of Judah

Modern society depends on technology workers and tradesmen to function. If they are not available, life becomes primitive. Almost all of the skilled workers in Judah were exiled to Babylon.

Jehoiachin reigned in Judah in 598 BC for three months.[15] He was deposed by Nebuchadnezzar, King of Babylon, and exiled to Babylon as a prisoner. In his thirty-seventh year of exile, he was released from prison and given a seat of honor by the new king of Babylon.

---

[15] 2 Kings 24:8–16; 25:27–30.

[King Jehoiachin] did what was evil in the Lord's sight just as his father had done.

At that time the servants of King Nebuchadnezzar of Babylon marched up to Jerusalem, and the city came under siege. King Nebuchadnezzar of Babylon came to the city while his servants were besieging it. King Jehoiachin of Judah, along with his mother, his servants, his commanders, and his officials, surrendered to the king of Babylon...

[Nebuchadnezzar] deported all Jerusalem and all the commanders and all the best soldiers—ten thousand captives including all the craftsmen and metalsmiths. Except for the poorest people of the land, no one remained.

2 Kings 24:9–14 (CSB)

During his short reign, King Jehoiachin continued the idolatry of his father. The Lord's judgment against Judah continued especially against the elite class who were the first to be deported.

Spiritual leaders and teachers bear special responsibility for those under their care.[16]

And you have forgotten the exhortation that addresses you as sons: My son, do not take the Lord's discipline lightly or lose heart when you are reproved by him, for the Lord disciplines the one he loves and punishes every son he receives. Endure suffering as discipline: God is dealing with you as sons. For what son is there that a father does not discipline?

Hebrews 12:5–7 (CSB)

The Lord disciplines his children and his judgment of sin is guaranteed. The Lord corrects me, so I don't keep going on the wrong path.

PRAYER: Lord, thank you for your love which disciplines me whenever I need it. Amen.

---

[16]James 3:1.

Zedekiah, son of Josiah, King of Judah

Popular culture exalts rebels. They become celebrities. But the consequences are often tragic. Zedekiah's rebellion cost him his kingdom.

Zedekiah reigned in Judah from about 597 to 586 BC.[17] He was made king by Nebuchadnezzar, King of Babylon. He died in Babylon.

> Zedekiah did what was evil in the Lord's sight just as Jehoiakim had done. Because of the Lord's anger, it came to the point in Jerusalem and Judah that he finally banished them from his presence. Then Zedekiah rebelled against the king of Babylon...
>
> The Chaldeans seized the king [Zedekiah] and brought him up to the king of Babylon at Riblah, and they passed sentence on him. They slaughtered Zedekiah's sons before his eyes. Finally, the king of Babylon blinded Zedekiah, bound him in bronze chains, and took him to Babylon.
>
> 2 Kings 24:19–20; 25:6–7 (CSB)

Zedekiah continued the idolatry of his brother Jehoiakim. Judah's sin reached its ultimate consequence. The fall and destruction of Jerusalem marked the end of Judah's existence as a nation and completed the Lord's judgment against Judah. Almost everyone was deported to Babylon except for a few of the very poorest farmers.

The exile to Babylon purged idolatry from Judah's national identity. Too often Christians dedicate themselves to modern idols. We need to purge idolatry too.

> I say this and testify in the Lord: You should no longer walk as the Gentiles do, in the futility of their thoughts.
>
> Ephesians 4:17 (CSB)

---

[17]2 Kings 24:17–25:7.

Zedekiah, son of Josiah, King of Judah

PRAYER: Lord, I repent of paying attention to a secular worldview. Help me recognize it whenever it creeps into my life. Amen.

8

A house in captivity

When I light a firecracker, the fuse may burn slowly, but then suddenly it explodes. Israel and Judah had a slow fuse.

The era of the house divided saw the people disobey the law given to Moses more and more. The Lord's prophets continued to call for repentance, but the people continued to worship idols. Eventually, Israel and Judah were deported from their land into captivity and their nations disappeared. This chapter has devotional meditations on why they were deported, and God's future plan for them.

Israel into captivity

Why did the Lord allow the northern kingdom of Israel to be conquered by Assyria and then deported into captivity?[1] The following lessons of their time are applicable to local churches today.

Israel worshiped like the Canaanites

The invasion of Canaan by Joshua and the Israelites was God's judgment for the Canaanites' sin. Israel did the same things.

> [Israel] lived according to the customs of the nations that the Lord had dispossessed before the Israelites

---

[1] 2 Kings 17:7–23.

and according to what the kings of Israel did. The Israelites secretly did things against the Lord their God that were not right. They built high places in all their towns from watchtower to fortified city. They set up for themselves sacred pillars and Asherah poles on every high hill and under every green tree. They burned incense there on all the high places just like the nations that the Lord had driven out before them had done. They did evil things, angering the Lord. They served idols, although the Lord had told them, "You must not do this."

2 Kings 17:8–12 (CSB)

Jeroboam and the people built shrines for worship on many high places and under trees just like the Canaanites. They set up sacred pillars (idols) and burned incense there. They also set up carved poles dedicated to the ancient fertility goddess Asherah. Worship included sexual immorality and prostitution. The kings and the people continued to worship on high places throughout the era of the house divided.

Jesus warned the church in Pergamum,[2] because some of their people held to the teaching of Balaam, namely, worshiping idols and sexual immorality.[3] In ancient times, eating meat offered to idols and sexual immorality were part of the ritual of idol worship. Some in Pergamum were doing these things just like the people in Israel. The examples of ancient Israel and Pergamum apply when church goers pursue modern idols or engage in sexual immorality. The Lord still calls for repentance today.

PRAYER: Lord, I will avoid modern idols and sexual immorality in all its forms. Amen.

Jeroboam made two gold calf idols

Jeroboam told the people that the gold calves were the gods that freed them from Egypt instead of the Lord whose temple was in

---

[2]Revelation 2:14–16.

[3]During the Exodus, the prophet Balaam showed Balak, king of Moab, how to corrupt the Israelites. Numbers 25:1–3.

Jerusalem.

> [Israel] abandoned all the commands of the Lord their God. They made cast images for themselves, two calves, and an Asherah pole...
> When the Lord tore Israel from the house of David, Israel made Jeroboam son of Nebat king. Then Jeroboam led Israel away from following the Lord and caused them to commit grave sin. The Israelites persisted in all the sins that Jeroboam committed and did not turn away from them.
>
> 2 Kings 17:16,21–22 (CSB)

Jeroboam set up the gold calves inside his domain, so the people would not travel to Jerusalem. Worshiping the gold calf idols was a substitute for proper worship of the Lord in Jerusalem. All the kings of Israel and the people continued the "sin of Jeroboam, son of Nebat," namely, worshiping the gold calves, until they were deported into captivity.

Jesus told the church in Ephesus to repent, because they had left their first love, the Lord himself.[4] The examples of Israel and Ephesus apply to any church today who has let other things capture their love. Loving anything above the Lord is like Israel worshiping gold calf idols. Nothing can substitute for the one true God. The Lord still calls for repentance today.

> PRAYER: Lord, loving you is my highest priority. Amen.

Jezebel introduced worship of Baal

King Ahab married a pagan princess, Jezebel, who introduced worship of her god, Baal. She also institutionalized worship of Baal and Asherah by financially supporting hundreds of pagan priests and building temples in the capital city, Samaria.

The people continued to worship Baal even after Elijah showed Baal was powerless at the contest on Mount Carmel. Baal

---

[4]Revelation 2:4–5.

worship was finally eliminated from Israel by Jehu when he over-threw Ahab's son King Joram.

Jesus told the church in Thyatira that he knew all about a corrupt leader who was like Jezebel in ancient Israel.[5] She was misleading the church into sexual immorality and eating food offered to idols. Sexual immorality was parallel to the worship of Asherah. Eating food offered to idols represented idol worship, such as worshiping Baal. Jesus promised to judge her and her followers. He told those who had not followed her to hold on to what they have. Some churches today have corrupt leaders. Eventually, scandals are revealed. Jesus has the same message today for those faced with corrupt leaders, "Hang on to what is good!"

> PRAYER: Lord, I will hold on to what is good, even when there is a scandal. Amen.

Israel practiced occult arts

Moses had strictly warned the Israelites against occult practices, which were common among the surrounding nations. However, Israel did them anyway.

> [Israel] bowed in worship to all the stars in the sky and served Baal. They sacrificed their sons and daughters in the fire and practiced divination and interpreted omens. They devoted themselves to do what was evil in the Lord's sight and angered him.
>
> Therefore, the Lord was very angry with Israel, and he removed them from his presence.
>
> 2 Kings 17:16–18 (CSB)

Besides worshiping idols, the kings and people in Israel sacrificed their sons and daughters in fire, worshiped the stars, practiced divination, and interpreted omens.

Jesus warned the church in Sardis, because they had a good reputation, but the church was actually spiritually dead.[6] What

---

[5]Revelation 2:20–25.
[6]Revelation 3:1–3.

little remained of spiritual life was about to die. Some churches today are spiritually dead, just going through the motions of religion without living faith. When there is no relationship with the Lord, church goers easily fall for approving of abortion, following horoscopes, studying astrology, and practicing Hindu, Buddhist, or Native American rituals. The Lord still calls for repentance today.

> PRAYER: Lord, whenever I see spiritual death, I will try to stir up any remaining life. Amen.

Israel rejected the Lord's covenant

The people of Israel stubbornly rejected the Lord's prophets who kept telling them to repent.

> This disaster, [Israel being deported,] happened because the people of Israel sinned against the Lord their God who had brought them out of the land of Egypt from the power of Pharaoh king of Egypt and because they worshiped other gods...
>
> Still, the Lord warned Israel and Judah through every prophet and every seer, saying, "Turn from your evil ways and keep my commands and statutes according to the whole law I commanded your ancestors and sent to you through my servants the prophets."
>
> But they would not listen. Instead they became obstinate like their ancestors who did not believe the Lord their God. They rejected his statutes and his covenant he had made with their ancestors and the warnings he had given them. They followed worthless idols and became worthless themselves, following the surrounding nations the Lord had commanded them not to imitate...
>
> Finally, the Lord removed Israel from his presence just as he had declared through all his servants the prophets. So Israel has been exiled to Assyria from their homeland to this very day.
>
> 2 Kings 17:7,13–15,23 (CSB)

Each of the kings of Israel from Jeroboam to Hoshea sinned against the Lord. The people followed the lead of their kings. The people of Israel adopted the idols of the surrounding nations and worshiped them. They also did evil things such as murder, theft, and oppressing the poor. The prophets Elijah, Elisha, and others warned them to repent over and over. Eventually, the Lord's patience ran out.

When churches today do similar things, such as rejecting the teachings of the Bible, adopting the prevailing culture, and approving of corrupt practices, the consequences will be the same. Like ancient Israel, Jesus warned the church in Ephesus, "I will come to you and remove your lampstand from its place, unless you repent."[7]

PRAYER: Lord, I pray that my church and the churches in my city will reject the prevailing culture. Amen.

Judah into captivity

Why did the Lord allow the southern kingdom of Judah to be conquered by Babylon and then deported into captivity?

During the exodus led by Moses, the Lord made a covenant with the Israelites at Mount Sinai (Horeb).[8] After wandering in the wilderness, the covenant between the Lord and the Israelites was renewed just before they entered Canaan.[9] Moses wrote the terms of the covenant on a scroll(s).[10]

Hundreds of years later, the forgotten scroll of the law of Moses was found during temple renovation and was read to King Josiah.[11] He knew Judah had sinned and deserved the curses spelled out in Deuteronomy. He repented on behalf of the nation. Josiah sent his officials to the prophetess Huldah to learn what the Lord would say.

---

[7]Revelation 2:5 (CSB).
[8]Exodus 19:1–24:11.
[9]Deuteronomy 27:1–30:20.
[10]Tradition attributes to Moses the books of Genesis through Deuteronomy.
[11]2 Kings 22:11–20.

She told them why the curses in Deuteronomy were going to be fulfilled.

> This is what the Lord says: I am about to bring disaster on this place and on its inhabitants, fulfilling all the words of the book that the king of Judah has read, because they have abandoned me and burned incense to other gods in order to anger me with all the work of their hands. My wrath will be kindled against this place, and it will not be quenched.
>
> 2 Kings 22:16–17 (CSB)

She also told Josiah that because he humbled himself before the Lord, the disaster would not happen in his lifetime.

The Scripture does not say exactly which passages were read to Josiah. Let us look at some of the renewed covenant in Deuteronomy Josiah may have heard read.

What had the people of Judah done?

Josiah recognized Judah had done what Deuteronomy predicted.

> These are the words of the covenant that the Lord commanded Moses to make with the Israelites in the land of Moab, in addition to the covenant he had made with them at Horeb...
>
> All the nations will ask, 'Why has the Lord done this to this land? Why this intense outburst of anger?'
>
> Then people will answer, 'It is because they abandoned the covenant of the Lord, the God of their ancestors, which he had made with them when he brought them out of the land of Egypt. They began to serve other gods, bowing in worship to gods they had not known—gods that the Lord had not permitted them to worship.'
>
> Deuteronomy 29:1,24–26 (CSB)

Like the northern kingdom of Israel, the people of Judah broke the covenant by worshiping other gods throughout the years, even though the Lord's temple was in Jerusalem. This broke the first commandment.[12] Breaking the rest of the Law followed from that.

Like ancient Judah, there are many idols in modern culture. Church goers, like everyone else, work hard to achieve worldly success in various areas, such as money, career, sports, hobbies, fame, sexuality, influence, and political power. If church goers today give their allegiance to the idols of our culture, disaster will follow.

PRAYER: Lord, I give my allegiance to you. Amen.

What did the Lord promise to do?

Josiah was alarmed that his domain was cursed and that they will be removed from the land.

> [People will say,] 'Therefore the Lord's anger burned against this land, and he brought every curse written in this book on it. The Lord uprooted them from their land in his anger, rage, and intense wrath, and threw them into another land where they are today.'
> Deuteronomy 29:27–28 (CSB)

The Lord promised to send them into captivity away from the land he had promised to their forefathers. Babylon fulfilled the prediction of conquest by a remote nation, who spoke a different language and ruthlessly slaughtered their enemies.[13]

The era of the house divided extended from the reign of King Rehoboam to that of King Zedekiah. Some of the kings did what was right and some were evil, like the kings of Israel. Worshiping the Lord in the temple in Jerusalem according to the law of Moses was important. When they sinned, prophets, such as Isaiah and Jeremiah, warned them to repent. Eventually, their sins were overwhelming and the Lord's patience ran out. He allowed Babylon to take them into captivity.

---

[12] Exodus 20:3–6 and Deuteronomy 6:4–5.
[13] Deuteronomy 28:49–50.

When Christians are not faithful, the Lord will discipline them.[14] Church history has many examples of churches and movements that have disappeared, or are just a shell today.[15] In some regions, conquerers or the government required people to follow a pagan religion, so many church goers complied. In other places, a movement died, because a charismatic leader died or people abandoned a heretic.

There may be challenges to my faith, sometimes from friends and sometimes from enemies. No matter what those around me do, maintaining my love for Jesus must be my top priority.

> See what great love the Father has given us that we should be called God's children—and we are! The reason the world does not know us is that it didn't know him.
>
> 1 John 3:1 (CSB)

> PRAYER: Lord, thank you for your love for me, so I can be a child of God. Amen.

After captivity

The independent nation of Israel was reestablished in AD 1948. Many saw this as a sign that God still cares for the descendants of the house divided, ancient Israel and Judah.

When their covenant was renewed before entering Canaan, the Lord predicted the Israelites would go into captivity because of their idolatry.[16] The Lord also revealed his plan for ending their captivity.

> When all these things happen to you—the blessings and curses I have set before you—and you come to your senses while you are in all the nations where the Lord your God has driven you, and you and your children return to the Lord your God and obey him with

---

[14]Hebrews 12:5–11.
[15]Revelation 2:5.
[16]Deuteronomy 29:1,27–28.

all your heart and all your soul by doing everything I am commanding you today, then he will restore your fortunes, have compassion on you, and gather you again from all the peoples where the Lord your God has scattered you.

Deuteronomy 30:1–3 (CSB)

Fulfillment of this prediction began when Cyrus, the Persian king, permitted a remnant to return to their homeland.[17] From that time on, the Jews never worshiped idols again. They may have had ethical lapses, political problems, and legalism, but they never resorted to worshiping other gods.

When I ponder how the Lord has been faithful to Israel and Judah in spite of their idolatry and other sins, I know he is also faithful to forgive my sins because of Jesus' death and resurrection.

PRAYER: Lord, I rest assured of your love for me in Christ Jesus. Amen.

. . . . The end . . . .

Please write a brief review of this book and post it at your on-line bookstore(s).

If you want to receive a weekly devotional meditation and occasional announcements, please send your email address to me at edward.allen1949@gmail.com
Your email will not be used for any other purpose.
— Ed

---

[17] 2 Chronicles 36:22–23.

Index

105

About the author

Edward B. Allen is the author of these books in daily devotional format.

- *A Slow Walk through Psalm 119: 90 Devotional Meditations*

- *A Slow Walk with James: 90 Devotional Meditations*

- *A Slow Walk with Peter: 275 Devotional Meditations*, including meditations on Jude

- *A Slow Walk during Christmas and Easter: Devotional Meditations for Advent and Lent*, including a chronological paraphrase of the Scriptures

- *A Slow Walk in a Houses Divided: 70 Devotional Meditations on 1 Kings and 2 Kings*

He is also the author of these other books which are straight reads with a devotional slant.

- *The Kingdom of Heaven: A Devotional Commentary on the Discourses of Jesus in Matthew*

- *Revelation: A Devotional Commentary*, including illustrations by Albrecht Dürer, fifteen meditations, and questions for personal or group study

- *Under the Sun and in the Kingdom: A Devotional Commentary on Ecclesiastes*

- *Love, Sex, Money, and Power: A Devotional Commentary*, including twelve meditations

111

- *Honest Questions: A Personal Commentary on Genesis 1 through 11*

- *Practical Faith: A Devotional Commentary*

He has led discussion Bible-study groups in evangelical churches for over 50 years, and has authored devotional articles for *The Upper Room* and *The Secret Place* magazines. He received a Ph.D. in Computer Science degree at Florida Atlantic University. He has had a career in software engineering and has authored or coauthored over 80 professional papers.

Made in the USA
Columbia, SC
14 November 2024

46401113R00070